Road & Destination Atlas
of
Loxahatchee Groves,
Royal Palm Beach,
and Wellington
Florida

INDEX

The Acreage
Westlake
West Palm Beach

Loxahatchee Groves
Royal Palm Beach

Wellington
Greenacres

1	2	3	4	5	6	7	8	9	10
11	12	13	14	15	16	17	18	19	20	21	22
23	24	25	26	27	28	29	30	31	32	33	34
35	36	37	38	39	40	41	42	43	44	45	46
47	48	49	50	51	52	53	54	55	56	57	58
59	60	61	62	63	64	65	66	67	68	69	70
71	72	73	74	75	76	77	78	79	80	81	82
	83	84	85	86	87	88	89	90	91	92	93
		94	95	96	97	98	99	100	101	102	103
				104	105	106	107	108	109	110	111
					112	113	114	115	116	117	118

0   1   2 mi

LEGEND

Points of Interest

- Arts Center
- ATM
- Bank
- Bar
- Bicycle Rental
- Cafe
- Cinema
- Clinic/Doctor
- College/University
- Community Center
- Fuel Station
- Library
- Pharmacy
- Place of Worship
- Police
- Post Office
- Pub/Bar
- Restaurant
- School
- Theater
- Restrooms
- Town Hall/Gov't Bldg

Areas of Interest

- Cemetery
- College/University
- Event Venue/Exhibition Center
- Hospital
- Parks

- Interstate Highways
- US Routes
- State Routes
- County Roads
- Local Roads
- Bicycle Paths
- Alleys/Paths
- Railroads
- County Boundaries
- City Boundaries
- Water

Orange Grove Blvd

Orange Grove Blvd

Orange Grove Blvd

44th Pl N

44th Pl N

44th Pl N

43rd Rd N

43rd Rd N

43rd Rd N

42nd Rd N

42nd Rd N

42nd Rd N

41st Rd N

41st Rd N

41st Rd N

The Acreage

40th Run N

40th Run N

40th Run N

180th St

Mandarin Blvd

3

Sycamore Dr W

2

4

Learwood Dr

38th Ln N

38th Ln N

38th Rd N

38th Rd N

38th Rd N

37th Pl N

37th Pl N

37th Pl N

36th Ct N

36th Ct N

36th Ct N

| 0 | 0.1 | 0.2 mi |

Pl N

3

35th Pl N

35th Pl N

35th Pl N

12

13

14

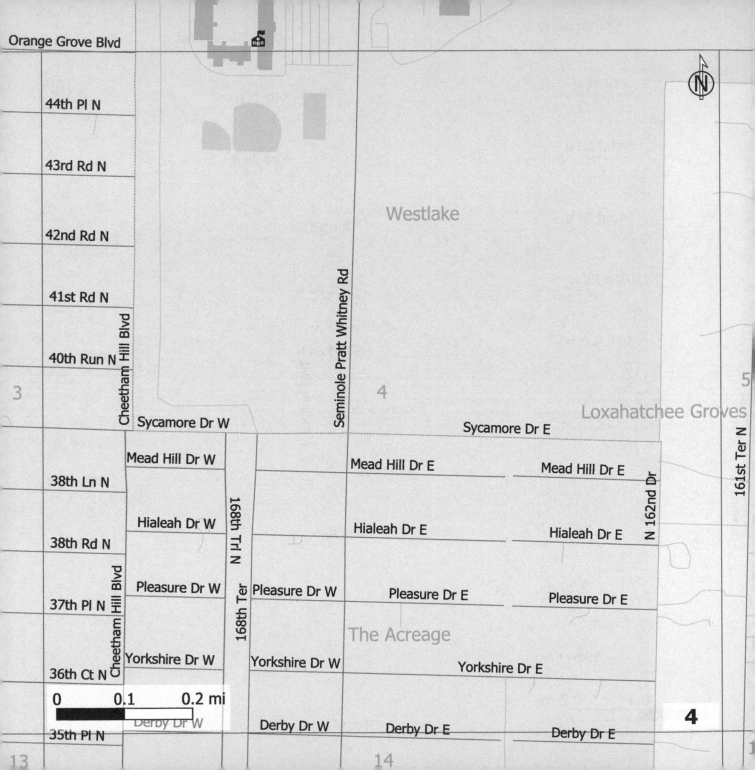

Westlake

44th St N

43rd Rd N

42nd Rd N

160th St N

42nd St N

Global Trl

161st Ter N

5

Ian Trl

6

41st Ct N   41st Ct N

Loxahatchee Groves

40th St N

North Rd

152nd St N

A Rd

B Rd

0   0.1   0.2 mi

Ferris Pl

5

4

15

16

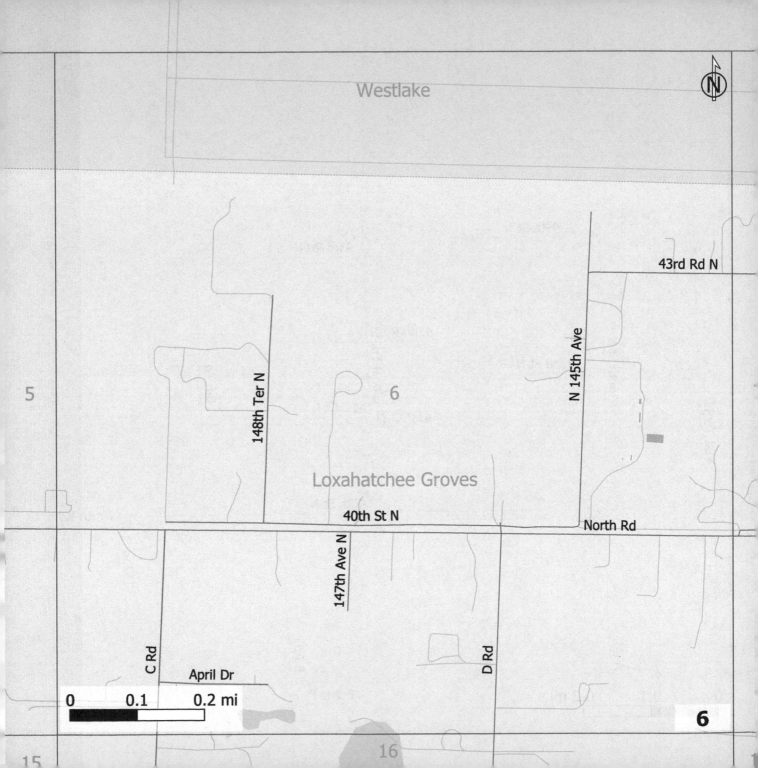

Westlake

43rd Rd N

N 145th Ave

148th Ter N

5

6

Loxahatchee Groves

40th St N

North Rd

147th Ave N

C Rd

D Rd

April Dr

0   0.1   0.2 mi

6

15   16

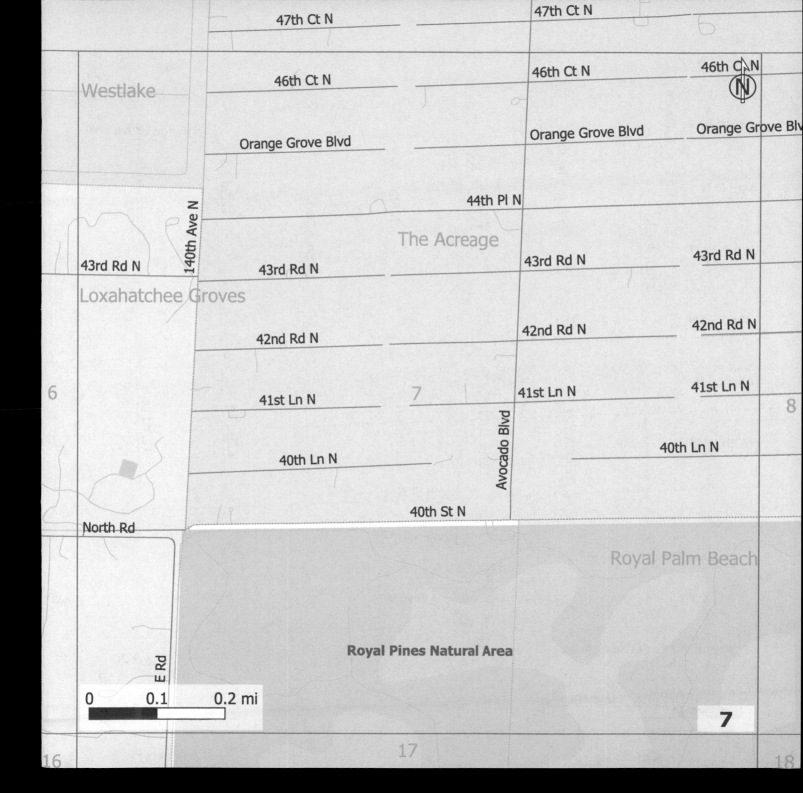

47th Ct N

47th Ct N

Westlake

46th Ct N

46th Ct N

46th Ct N

Orange Grove Blvd

Orange Grove Blvd

Orange Grove Blv

44th Pl N

The Acreage

140th Ave N

43rd Rd N

43rd Rd N

43rd Rd N

43rd Rd N

Loxahatchee Groves

42nd Rd N

42nd Rd N

42nd Rd N

6

7

41st Ln N

41st Ln N

41st Ln N

Avocado Blvd

40th Ln N

40th Ln N

8

40th St N

North Rd

Royal Palm Beach

E Rd

Royal Pines Natural Area

0   0.1   0.2 mi

7

16

17

18

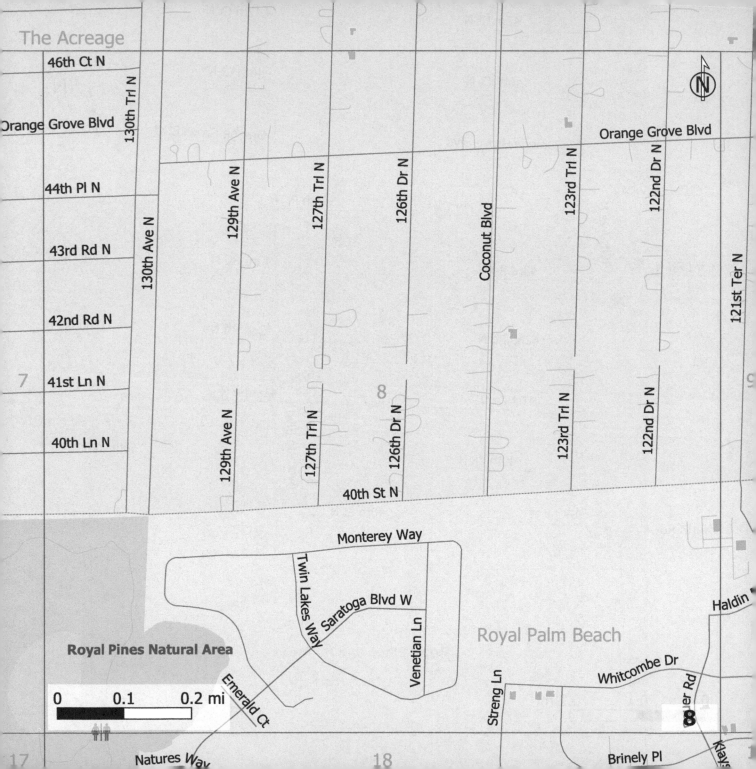

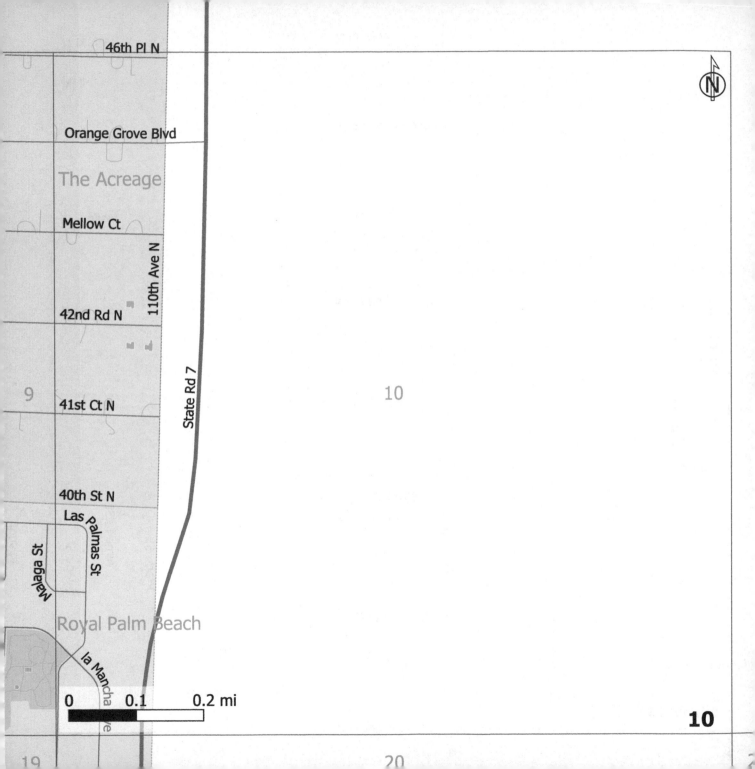

46th Pl N

Orange Grove Blvd

The Acreage

Mellow Ct

110th Ave N

42nd Rd N

9

State Rd 7

41st Ct N

40th St N

Las Palmas St

Malaga St

10

Royal Palm Beach

la Mancha

0   0.1   0.2 mi

10

19   20

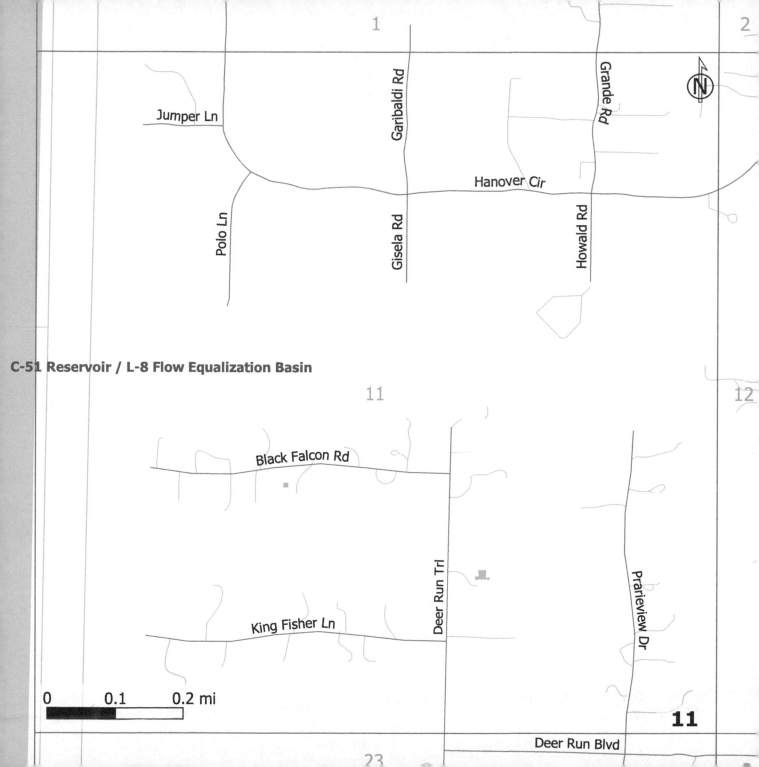

C-51 Reservoir / L-8 Flow Equalization Basin

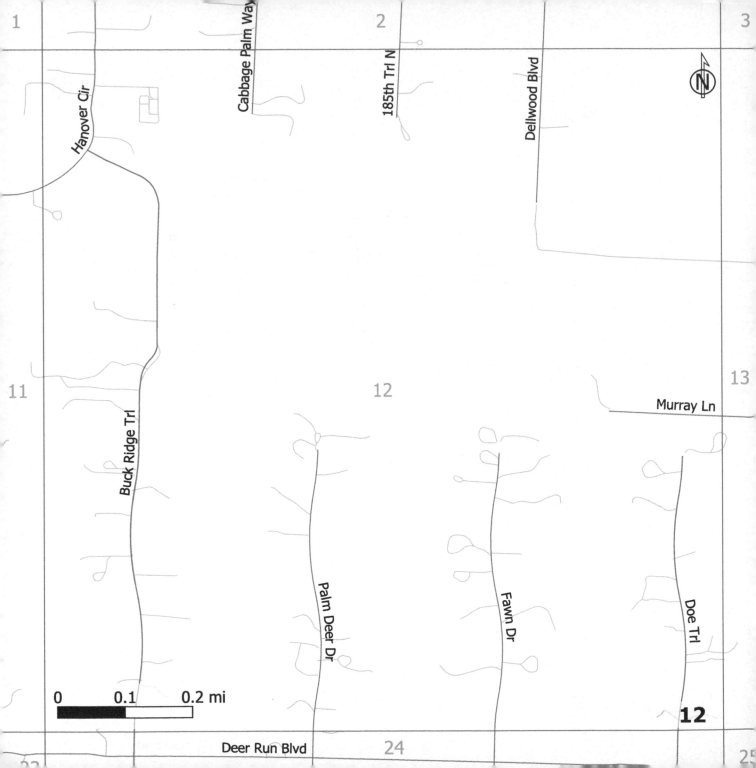

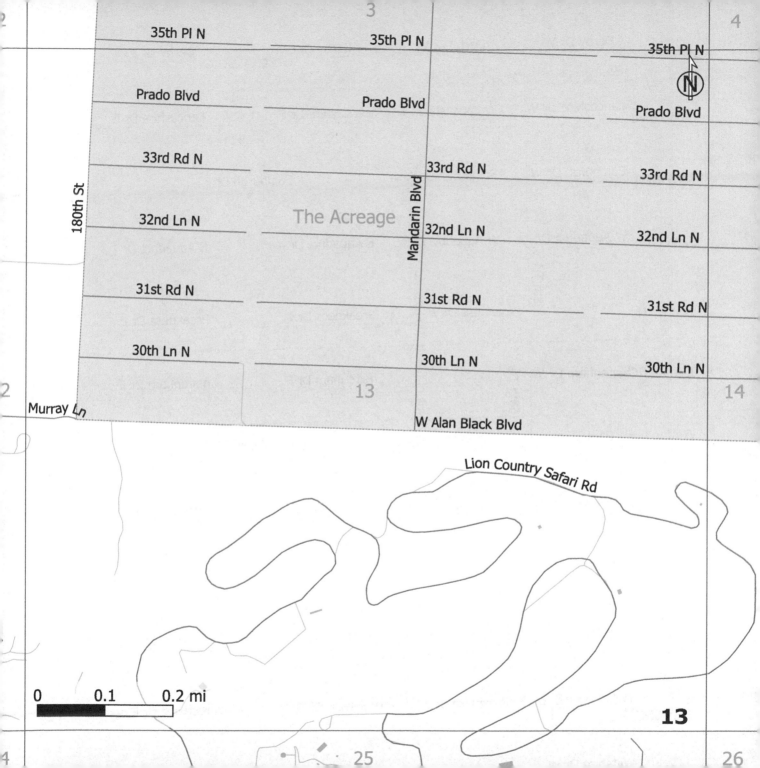

35th Pl N   35th Pl N   35th Pl N

Prado Blvd   Prado Blvd   Prado Blvd

33rd Rd N   33rd Rd N   33rd Rd N

The Acreage

32nd Ln N   32nd Ln N   32nd Ln N

Mandarin Blvd

31st Rd N   31st Rd N   31st Rd N

30th Ln N   30th Ln N   30th Ln N

180th St

Murray Ln

W Alan Black Blvd

Lion Country Safari Rd

3

4

2

2

13

14

25

26

13

0   0.1   0.2 mi

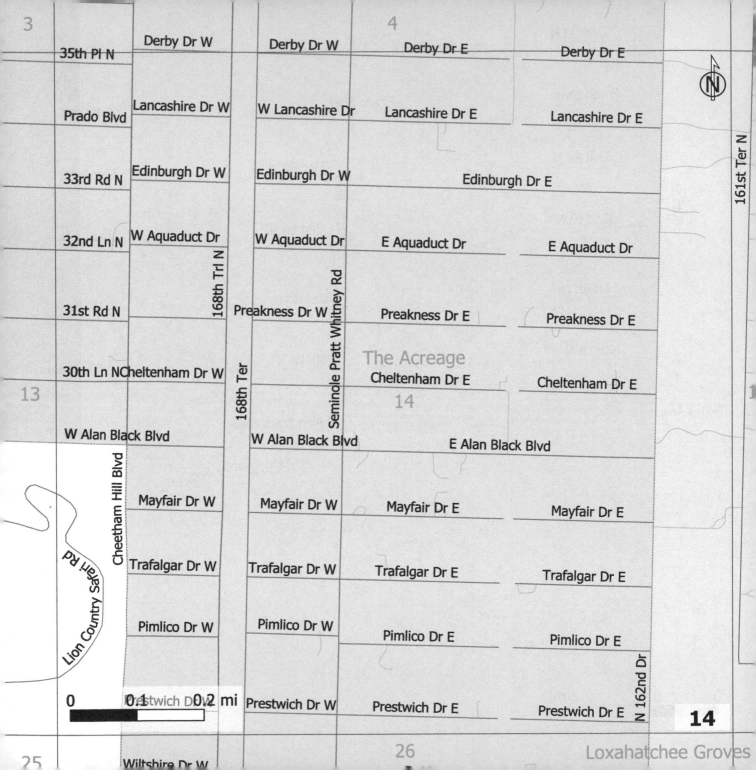

3

4

35th Pl N

Derby Dr W

Derby Dr W

Derby Dr E

Derby Dr E

N

Prado Blvd

Lancashire Dr W

W Lancashire Dr

Lancashire Dr E

Lancashire Dr E

161st Ter N

33rd Rd N

Edinburgh Dr W

Edinburgh Dr W

Edinburgh Dr E

32nd Ln N

W Aquaduct Dr

W Aquaduct Dr

E Aquaduct Dr

E Aquaduct Dr

168th Trl N

31st Rd N

Preakness Dr W

Preakness Dr E

Preakness Dr E

Seminole Pratt Whitney Rd

The Acreage

30th Ln N Cheltenham Dr W

168th Ter

Cheltenham Dr E

Cheltenham Dr E

13

14

W Alan Black Blvd

W Alan Black Blvd

E Alan Black Blvd

Cheetham Hill Blvd

Mayfair Dr W

Mayfair Dr W

Mayfair Dr E

Mayfair Dr E

Lion Country Safari Rd

Trafalgar Dr W

Trafalgar Dr W

Trafalgar Dr E

Trafalgar Dr E

Pimlico Dr W

Pimlico Dr W

Pimlico Dr E

Pimlico Dr E

N 162nd Dr

0   0.1   0.2 mi

Prestwich Dr W

Prestwich Dr W

Prestwich Dr E

Prestwich Dr E

14

25

Wiltshire Dr W

26

Loxahatchee Groves

4

5

Ferris Pl

6

N

161st Ter N

B Rd

B Rd

B Rd

B Rd

A Rd

14

15

16

Loxahatchee Groves

Steffan Ln

W A Rd

B Rd

28th Ln N

Lakeside Dr

Fortner Dr

Fortner Dr

0   0.1   0.2 mi

15

26

27

28

7

8

N

35th Pl N

Royal Palm Beach

Royal Pines Natural Area

6

E Rd

17

18

North Rd

Loxahatchee Groves

F Rd

0   0.1   0.2 mi
Paddle Foot

29

30

17 March Cir

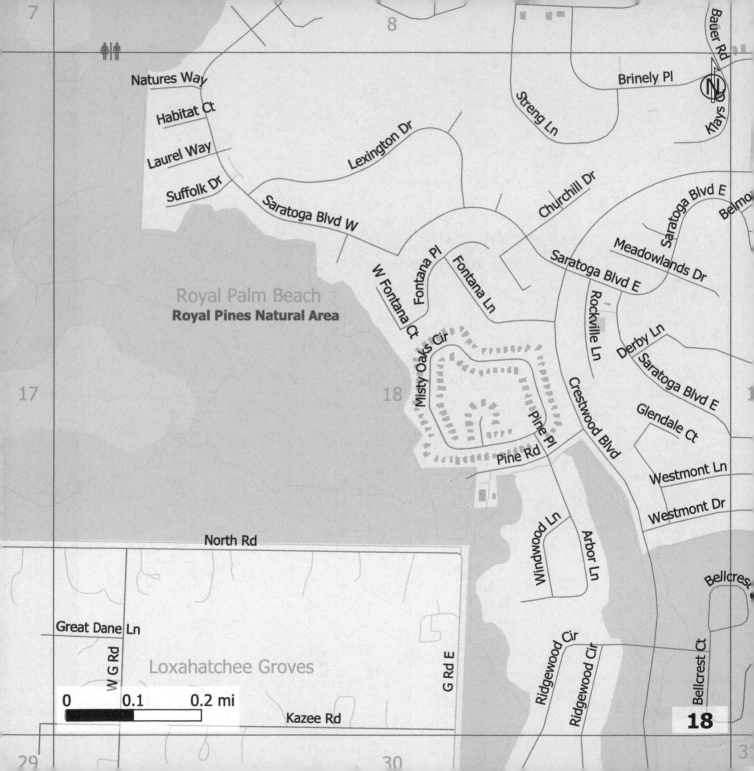

7

8

Natures Way

Habitat Ct

Laurel Way

Suffolk Dr

Lexington Dr

Saratoga Blvd W

Brinely Pl

Streng Ln

Bauer Rd

Krays

Churchill Dr

Saratoga Blvd E

Belmo

Meadowlands Dr

Saratoga Blvd E

Royal Palm Beach
Royal Pines Natural Area

W Fontana Ct

Fontana Pl

Fontana Ln

Saratoga Blvd E

Rockville Ln

Derby Ln

Saratoga Blvd E

Glendale Ct

17

18

Misty Oaks Cir

Pine Pl

Crestwood Blvd

Westmont Ln

Pine Rd

Westmont Dr

North Rd

Windpump Ln

Arbor Ln

Bellcres

Great Dane Ln

W G Rd

Loxahatchee Groves

G Rd E

Ridgewood Cir

Ridgewood Cir

Bellcrest Ct

0   0.1   0.2 mi

Kazee Rd

18

29

30

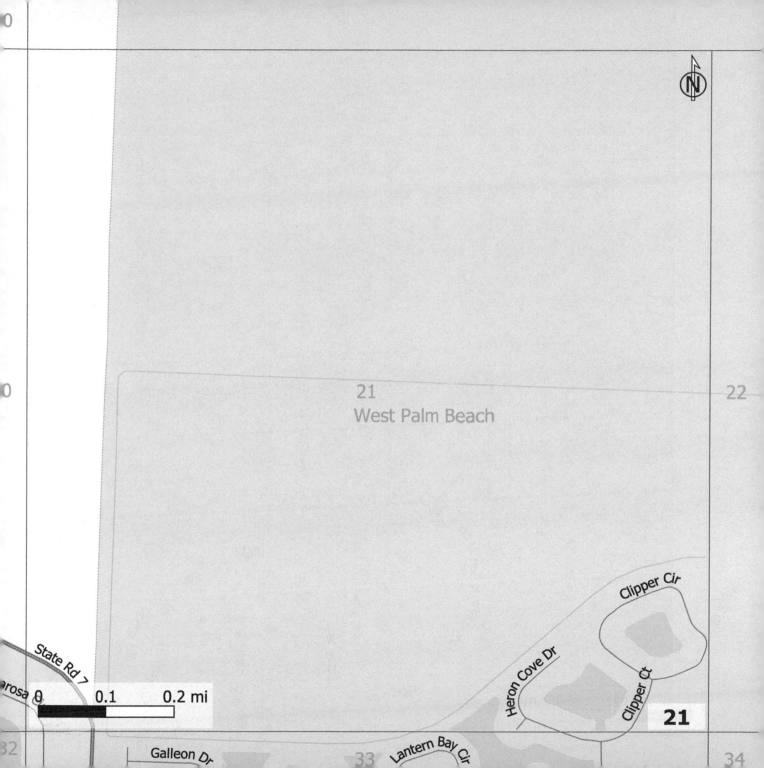

21
West Palm Beach

22

Clipper Cir

Heron Cove Dr

Clipper Ct

21

State Rd 7

arosa

0   0.1   0.2 mi

32

Galleon Dr

33   Lantern Bay Cir

34

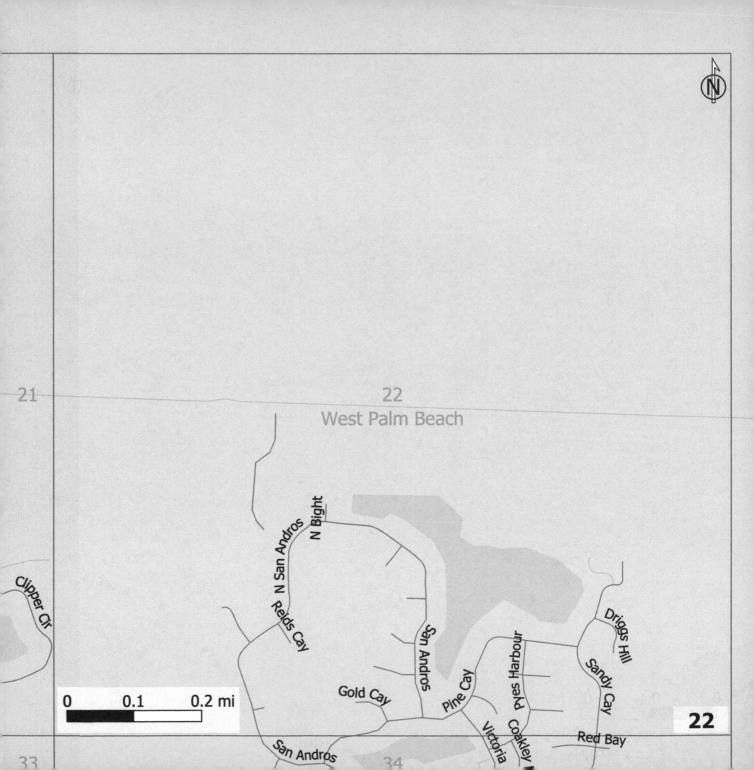

21

Clipper Cir

N San Andros

N Bight

N Reids Cay

Gold Cay

San Andros

Pine Cay

Coakley

Victoria

es Harbour

Driggs Hill

Sandy Cay

Red Bay

0   0.1   0.2 mi

San Andros

33

34

22

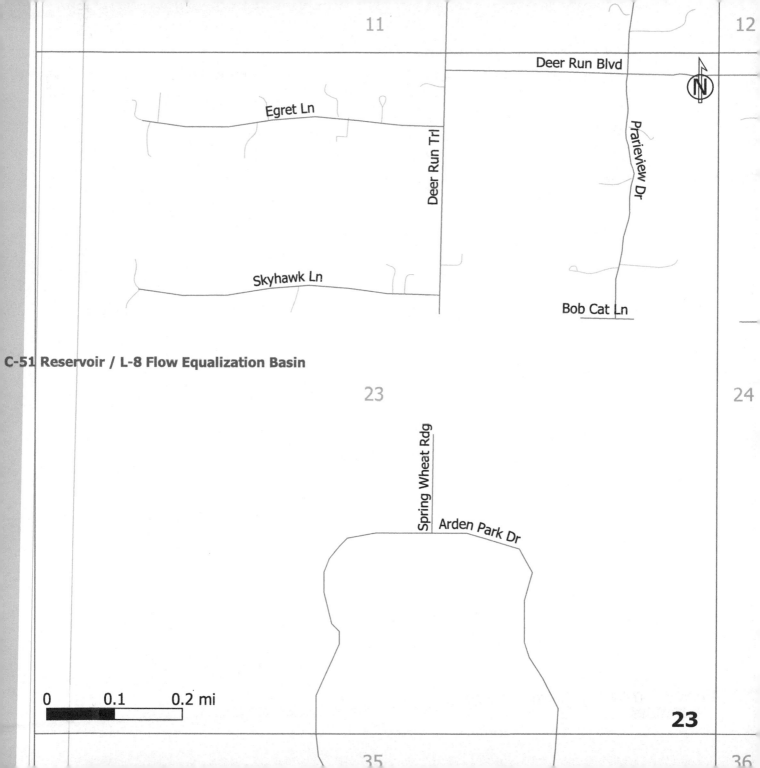

11

12

Deer Run Blvd

Egret Ln

Deer Run Trl

Praieview Dr

Skyhawk Ln

Bob Cat Ln

C-51 Reservoir / L-8 Flow Equalization Basin

23

24

Spring Wheat Rdg

Arden Park Dr

0   0.1   0.2 mi

23

35

36

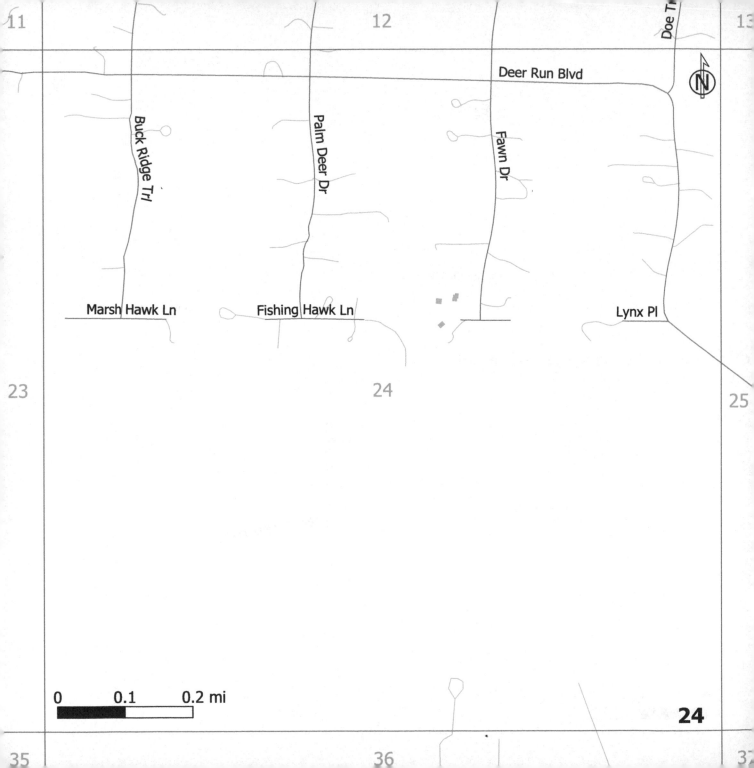

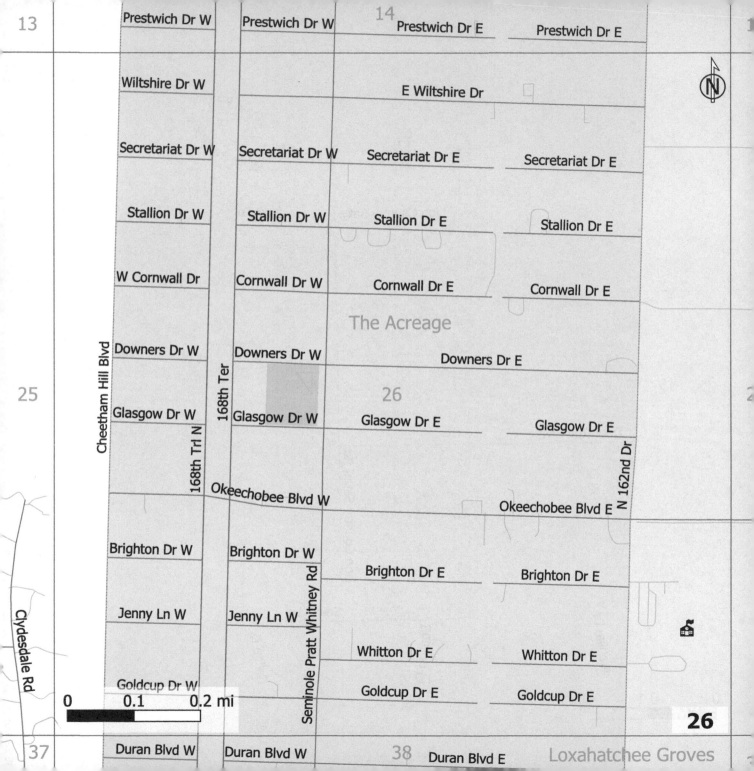

14

15

16

25th Pl N

Morrow Ct

Loxahatchee Groves

A Rd

26

27

B Rd

Shamrock Dr

28

Jewel Ln

keechobee Blvd E

Okeechobee Blvd

Sallys Aly

0   0.1   0.2 mi

17th Rd N

27

Timberlane Pl

C Rd

38

39

San Diego Dr

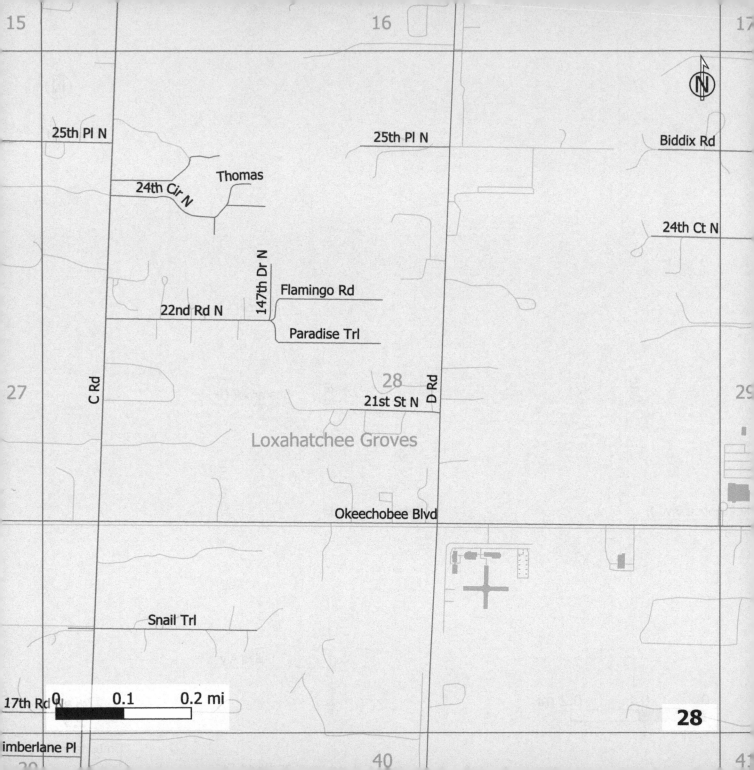

15

16

17

25th Pl N

25th Pl N

Biddix Rd

Thomas

24th Cir N

24th Ct N

147th Dr N

Flamingo Rd

22nd Rd N

Paradise Trl

C Rd

28

D Rd

27

29

21st St N

Loxahatchee Groves

Okeechobee Blvd

Snail Trl

17th Rd N

0   0.1   0.2 mi

28

imberlane Pl

30

40

4

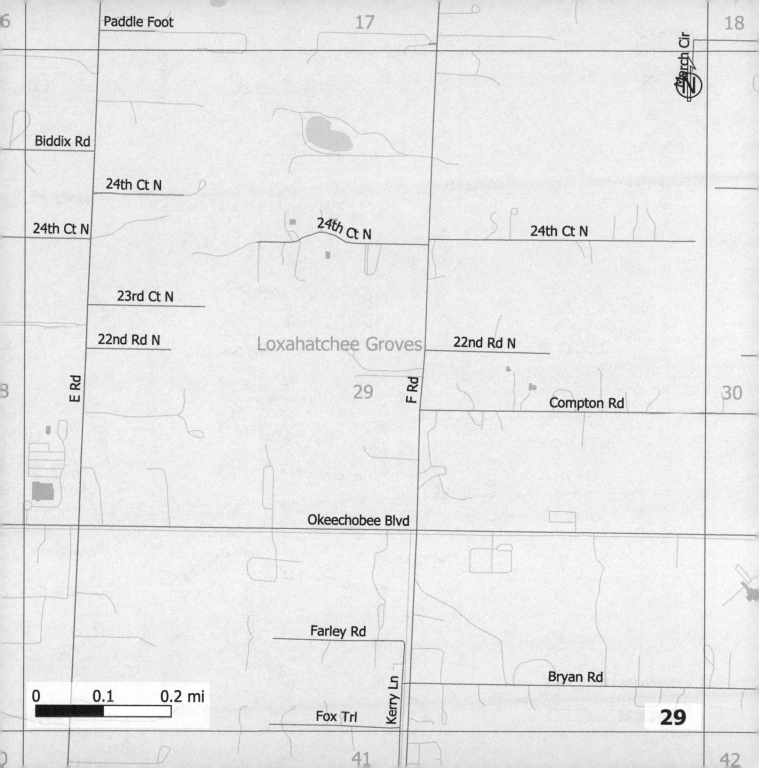

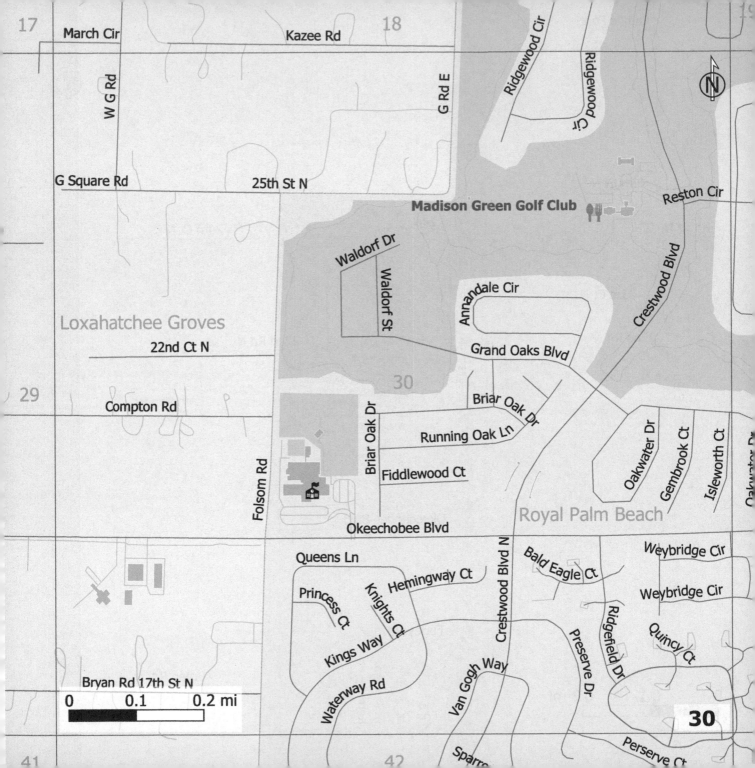

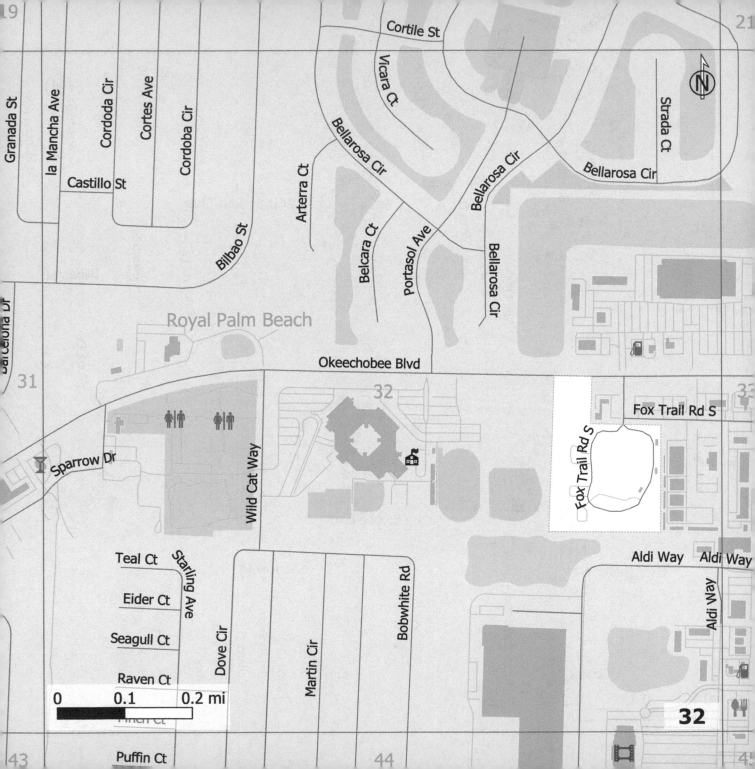

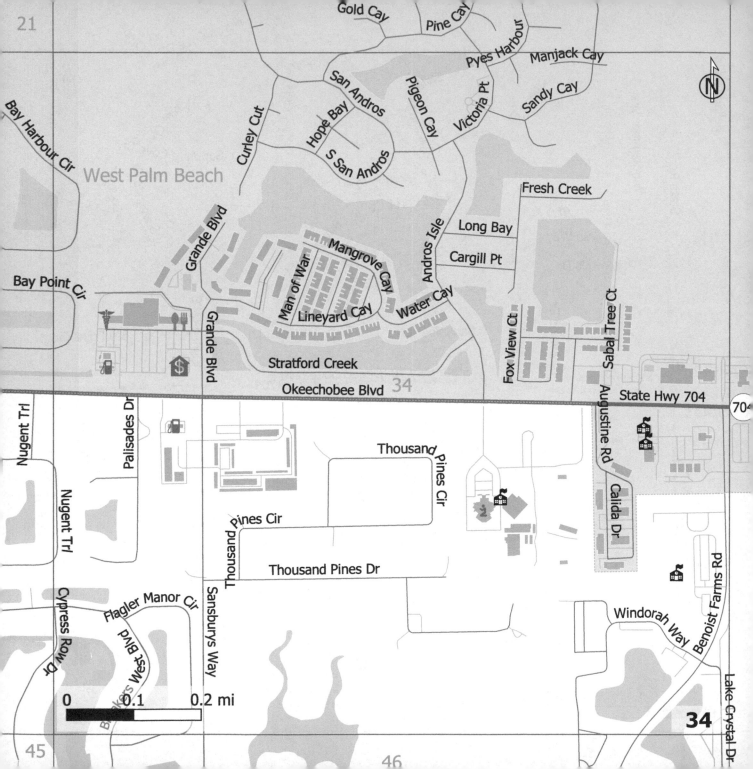

Gold Cay

Pine Cay

Pyes Harbour

Manjack Cay

Sandy Cay

Bay Harbour Cir

San Andros

Curley Cut

Hope Bay

Pigeon Cay

Victoria Pt

West Palm Beach

S San Andros

Fresh Creek

Long Bay

Andros Isle

Cargill Pt

Bay Point Cir

Grande Blvd

Mangrove Cay

Man of War

Lineyard Cay

Water Cay

Fox View Ct

Sabal Tree Ct

Grande Blvd

Stratford Creek

Okeechobee Blvd   34

State Hwy 704

Augustine Rd

704

Nugent Trl

Palisades Dr

Thousand Pines Cir

Nugent Trl

Pines Cir

Calida Dr

Thousand Pines Cir

Thousand Pines Dr

Cypress Row Dr

Flagler Manor Cir

Sansburys Way

Windorah Way

Benoist Farms Rd

Brokers West Blvd

Lake Crystal Dr

0   0.1   0.2 mi

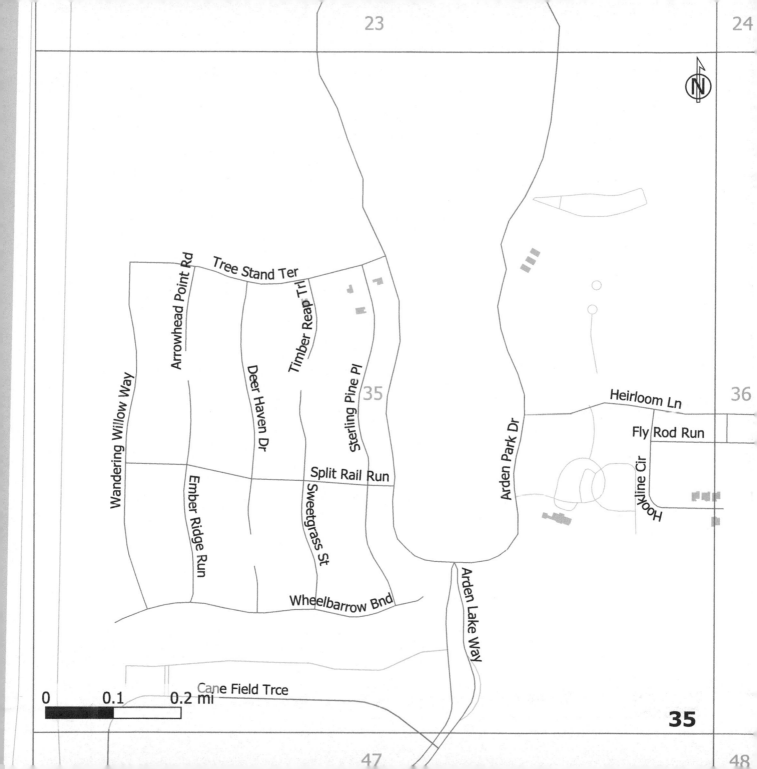

N

Arrowhead Point Rd

Tree Stand Ter

Timber Reap Trl

36

Heirloom Ln

Fly Rod Run

Deer Haven Dr

Sterling Pine Pl

35

Arden Park Dr

Hookline Cir

Wandering Willow Way

Split Rail Run

Ember Ridge Run

Sweetgrass St

Wheelbarrow Bnd

Arden Lake Way

Cane Field Trce

0   0.1   0.2 mi

35

23

24

25

35

36

37

Heirloom Ln

Fly Rod Run

Hookline Cir

0   0.1   0.2 mi

36

47

48

49

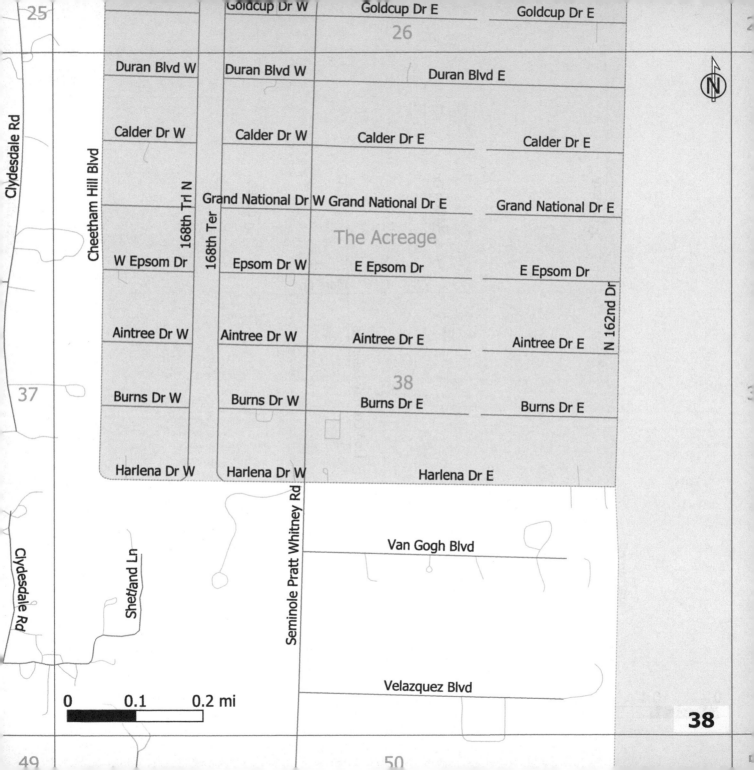

Goldcup Dr W | Goldcup Dr E | Goldcup Dr E

25

26

Clydesdale Rd

Cheetham Hill Blvd

Duran Blvd W | Duran Blvd W | Duran Blvd E

Calder Dr W | Calder Dr W | Calder Dr E | Calder Dr E

168th Trl N

168th Ter

Grand National Dr W | Grand National Dr E | Grand National Dr E

The Acreage

W Epsom Dr | Epsom Dr W | E Epsom Dr | E Epsom Dr

Aintree Dr W | Aintree Dr W | Aintree Dr E | Aintree Dr E

N 162nd Dr

37

38

Burns Dr W | Burns Dr W | Burns Dr E | Burns Dr E

Harlena Dr W | Harlena Dr W | Harlena Dr E

Shetland Ln

Seminole Pratt Whitney Rd

Van Gogh Blvd

Clydesdale Rd

Velazquez Blvd

0   0.1   0.2 mi

38

49

50

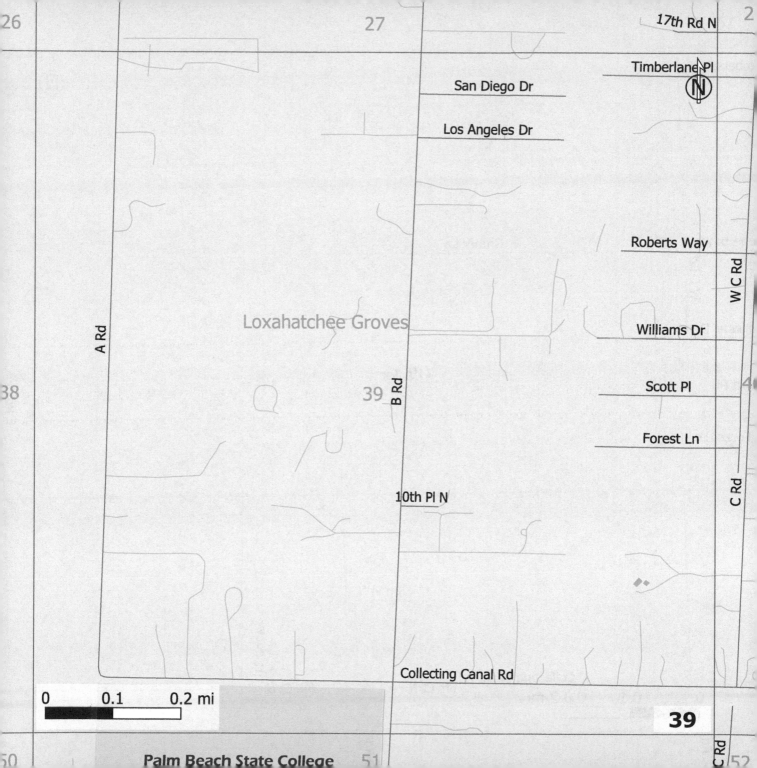

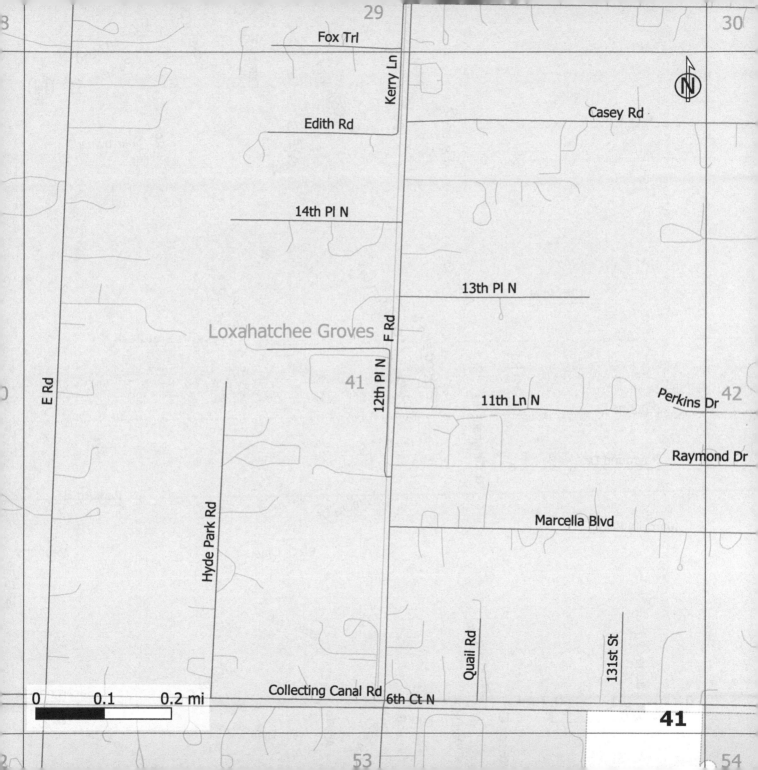

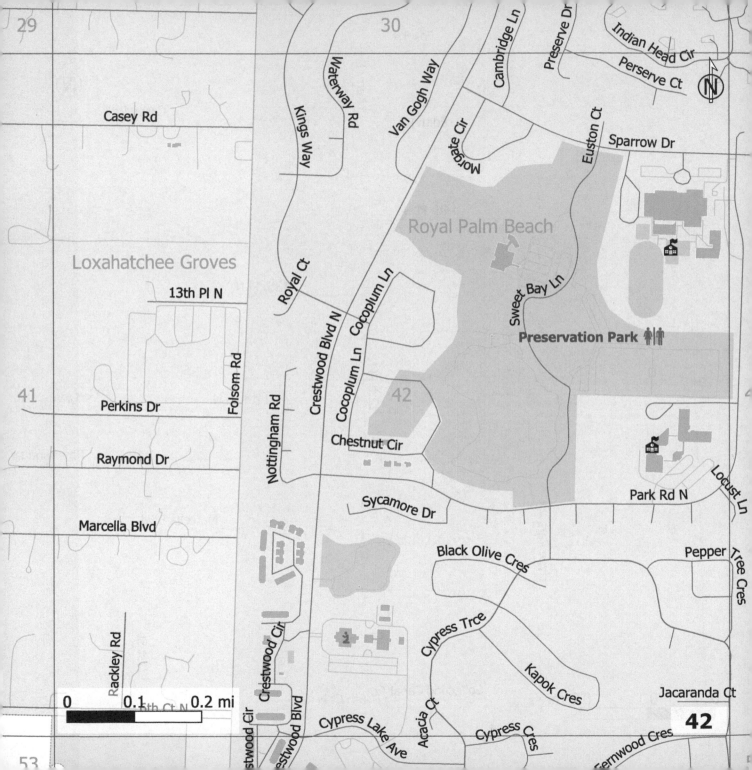

30

Casey Rd

Loxahatchee Groves

13th Pl N

41

Perkins Dr

Raymond Dr

Marcella Blvd

Cambridge Ln

Preserve Dr

Indian Head Cir

Perserve Ct

Van Gogh Way

Waterway Rd

Kings Way

Morgate Cir

Euston Ct

Sparrow Dr

Royal Palm Beach

Royal Ct

Cocoplum Ln

Cocoplum Ln

Crestwood Blvd N

Sweet Bay Ln

Preservation Park ♀♂

Nottingham Rd

42

Chestnut Cir

Park Rd N

Locust Ln

Sycamore Dr

Black Olive Cres

Pepper Tree Cres

Rackley Rd

Crestwood Cir

Cypress Tree

Cypress Trce

Kapok Cres

Jacaranda Ct

0   0.1 5th Ct N 0.2 mi

Crestwood Cir

Crestwood Blvd

Acacia Ct

Cypress Lake Ave

Cypress Cres

Fernwood Cres

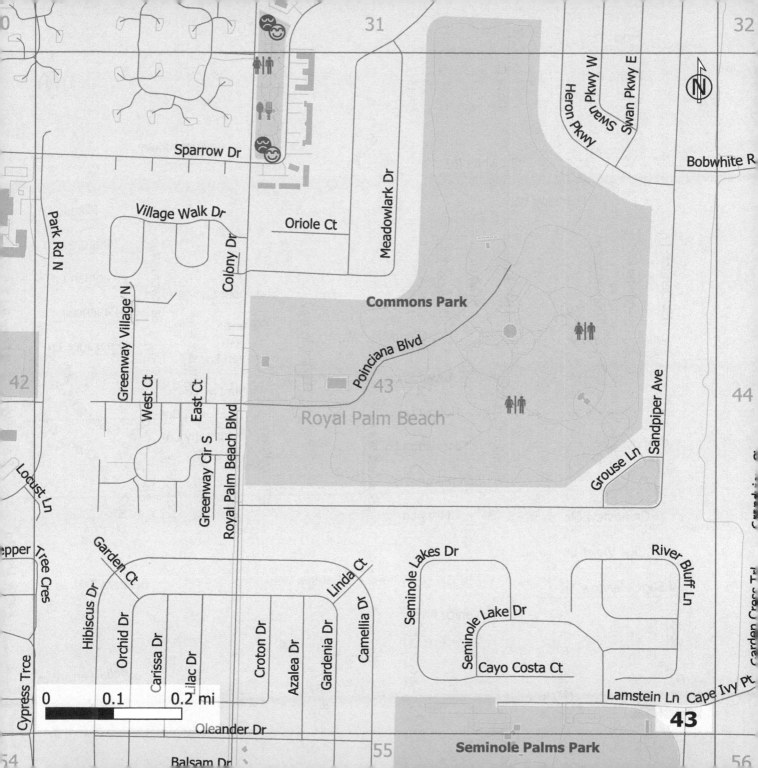

Swan Pkwy W

Swan Pkwy E

Heron Pkwy

Bobwhite R

Sparrow Dr

Meadowlark Dr

Village Walk Dr

Oriole Ct

Colony Dr

Park Rd N

Greenway Village N

Commons Park

West Ct

East Ct

Poinciana Blvd

42

43

44

Greenway Cir S

Royal Palm Beach Blvd

Royal Palm Beach

Sandpiper Ave

Grouse Ln

Locust Ln

Tree Cres

pepper

Garden Ct

Seminole Lakes Dr

River Bluff Ln

Hibiscus Dr

Orchid Dr

Carissa Dr

Lilac Dr

Linda Ct

Camellia Dr

Croton Dr

Azalea Dr

Gardenia Dr

Seminole Lake Dr

Garden Cres Trl

Cypress Trce

Cayo Costa Ct

Lamstein Ln Cape Ivy Pt

| 0 | 0.1 | 0.2 mi |

43

Oleander Dr

54

Balsam Dr

55

Seminole Palms Park

56

Gulfstream Way

Enclave Cir

Enclave Cir

Enclave Cir

Enclave Cir

Flagler Pkwy

The Breakers Rees Jones Course

ness Pkwy

kado Ln

fore Ln

man Ln

ence Ln

N State Rd 7

Breakers West Blvd

Breakers West Blvd

Mayacoo Lakes Blvd

rus Way

State Hwy 7 Range Line Rd

Sand Drift Way

45

Lytham Ct

Heathridge Dr

Mayacoo Lakes Blvd

Drury Pl

Belvedere Rd

7

Bellezza Ter

Royal Palm Beach

Fairgrounds Rd

Fairgrounds Rd

0   0.1   0.2 mi

5th Ave N

Fairgrounds

45

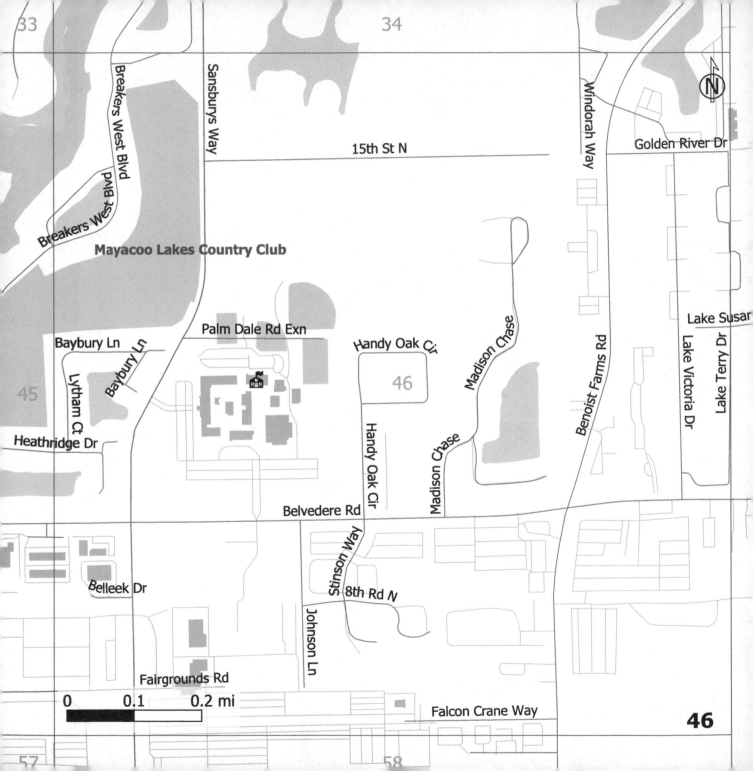

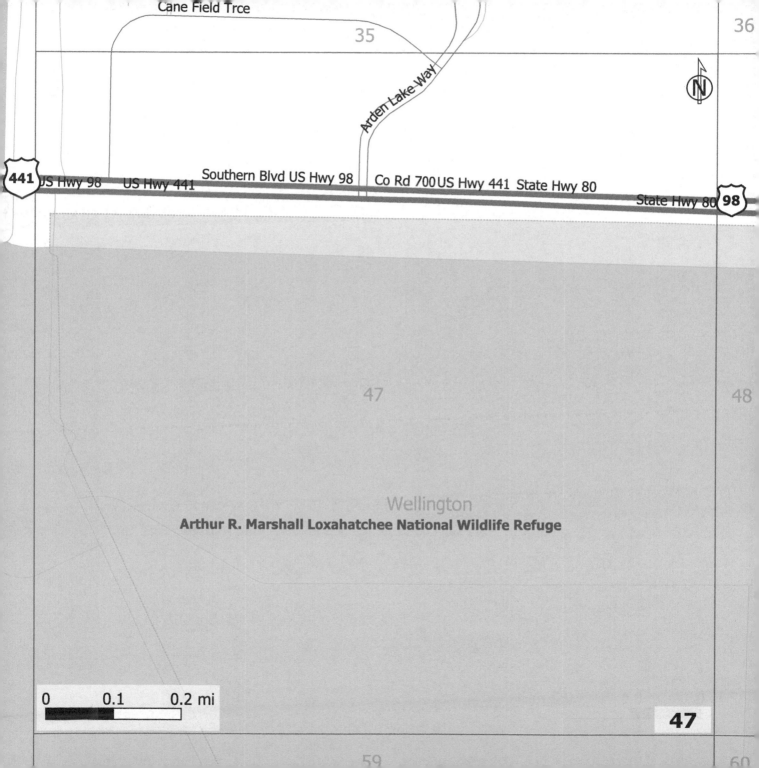

Cane Field Trce

35

36

Arden Lake Way

441 US Hwy 98 US Hwy 441 Southern Blvd US Hwy 98 Co Rd 700 US Hwy 441 State Hwy 80

State Hwy 80 98

47

48

Wellington

Arthur R. Marshall Loxahatchee National Wildlife Refuge

0 0.1 0.2 mi

47

59

60

35

36

3/

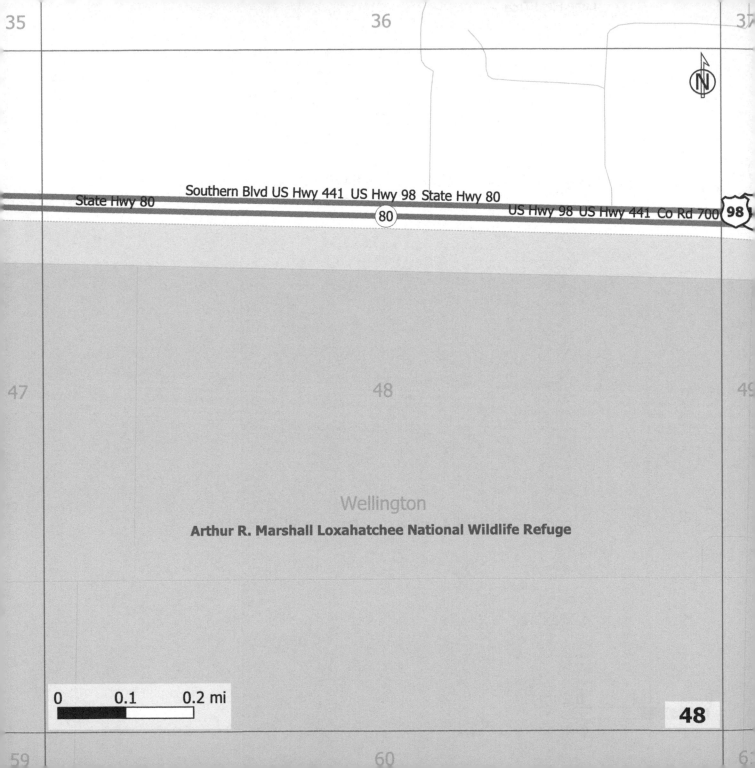

State Hwy 80

Southern Blvd US Hwy 441 US Hwy 98 State Hwy 80

US Hwy 98 US Hwy 441 Co Rd 700 98

80

47

48

49

Wellington

Arthur R. Marshall Loxahatchee National Wildlife Refuge

0   0.1   0.2 mi

48

59

60

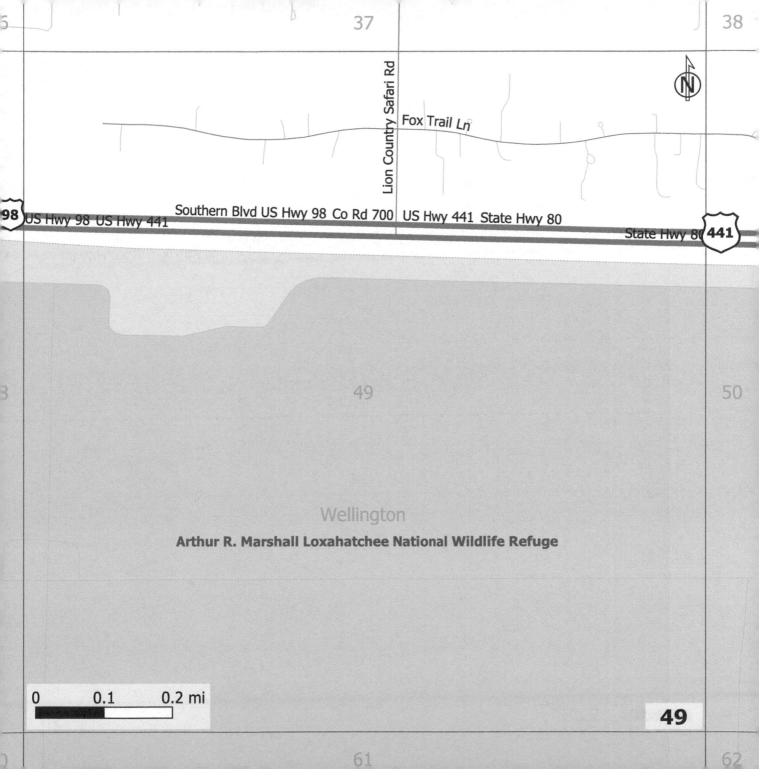

Lion County Safari Rd

Fox Trail Ln

98 US Hwy 98 US Hwy 441   Southern Blvd US Hwy 98 Co Rd 700   US Hwy 441 State Hwy 80

State Hwy 80 **441**

3   49   50

Wellington

Arthur R. Marshall Loxahatchee National Wildlife Refuge

0   0.1   0.2 mi

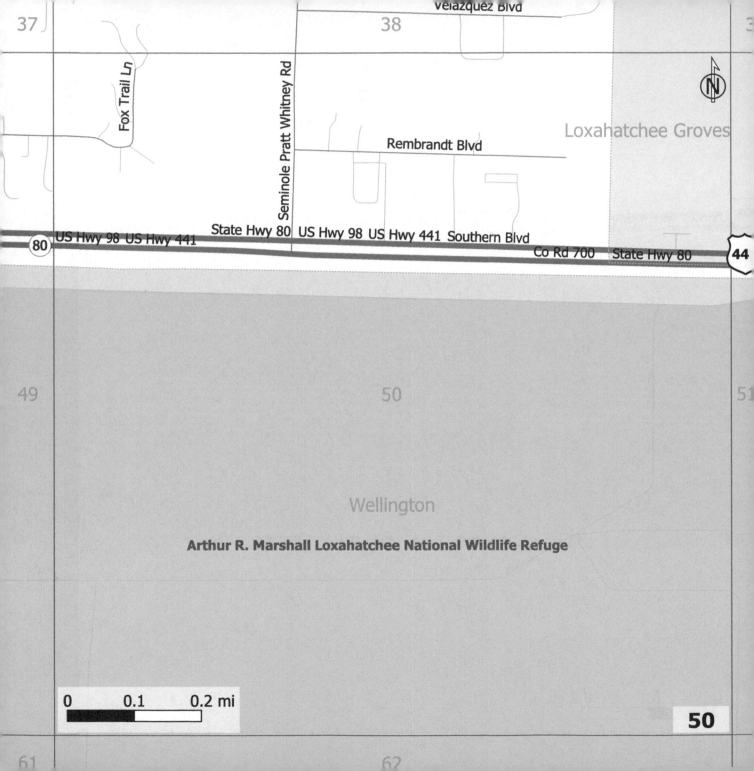

37

38

Velazquez Blvd

Fox Trail Ln

Seminole Pratt Whitney Rd

Loxahatchee Groves

Rembrandt Blvd

US Hwy 98 US Hwy 441   State Hwy 80 US Hwy 98 US Hwy 441 Southern Blvd

80   Co Rd 700   State Hwy 80   **44**

49

50

51

Wellington

Arthur R. Marshall Loxahatchee National Wildlife Refuge

| 0 | 0.1 | 0.2 mi |

50

61

62

Palm Beach State College

Loxahatchee Groves

B Rd

C Rd

N

Southern Blvd

80 US Hwy 441 US Hwy 98 US Hwy 441 Co Rd 700 US Hwy 98 Southern Blvd State Hwy 80 441 98

Glen Willow Ln

Whispering Willow Dr

Osley Farms Rd

Bent Creek Rd 51

52

Oak Chase Ct

Flying Cow Rd

Binks Forest Dr

Wellington

Binks Pointe Ter

Italian Cypress Way

Gulf Pine Cir

Haymarket C

Squire Dr

Cypress Green Cir

Cypress King

0   0.1   0.2 mi

Binks Forest Golf Club

Binks Estate Dr

Forest Glen

63

Farrier

51

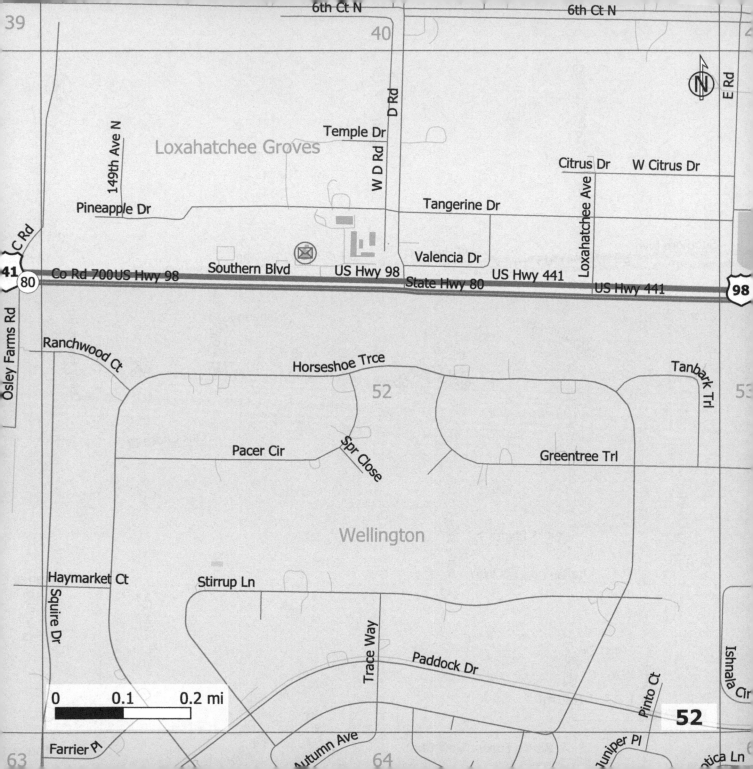

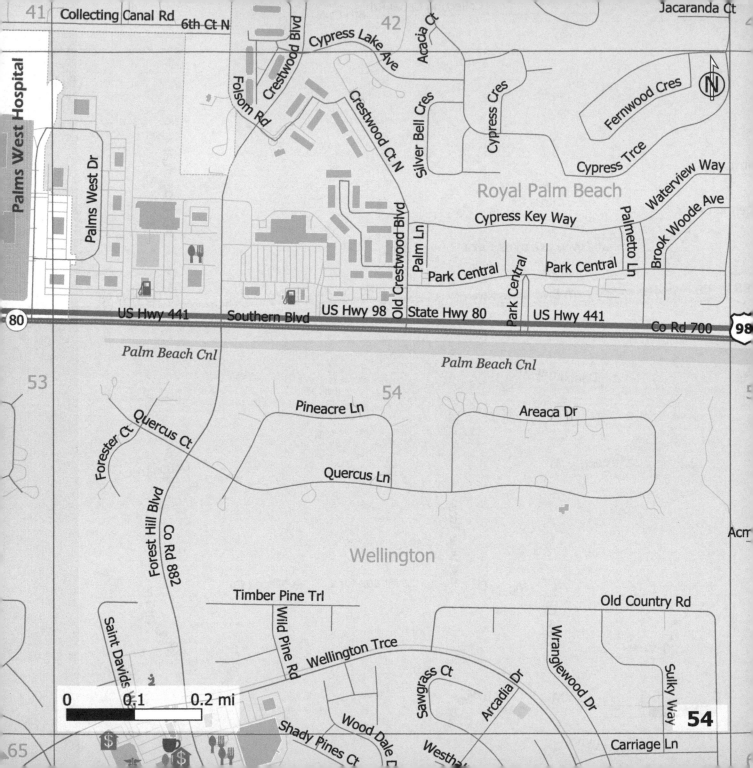

45

46 Falcon Crane Way

N

Sansburys Way

Benoist Farms Rd

Kelly Dr

Bama Ln

Gator Ln

Wallis Rd

Hooper Rd

57 US Hwy 98 Southern Blvd US Hwy 98 Co Rd 700 State Hwy 80 Southern Blvd

58

State Hwy 80 98

Palm Beach Cnl

Belle Grove Ln

Whispering Oak Way

Belle Grove Ln

Butler Greenwood Dr

Benoist Farms Rd S

Mahogany Ln

Tally Ho Ln

Elle

Palm Beach Plantation Blvd

Lyons Rd

Atwell Dr

Mariposa Grove Cir

1st Ln S

Marginal Rd

Safe Haven D

Florida's Tpke Florida'

0   0.1   0.2 mi

8th Ter S

Pioneer Ln

Pioneer Rd

58

Mozart

70

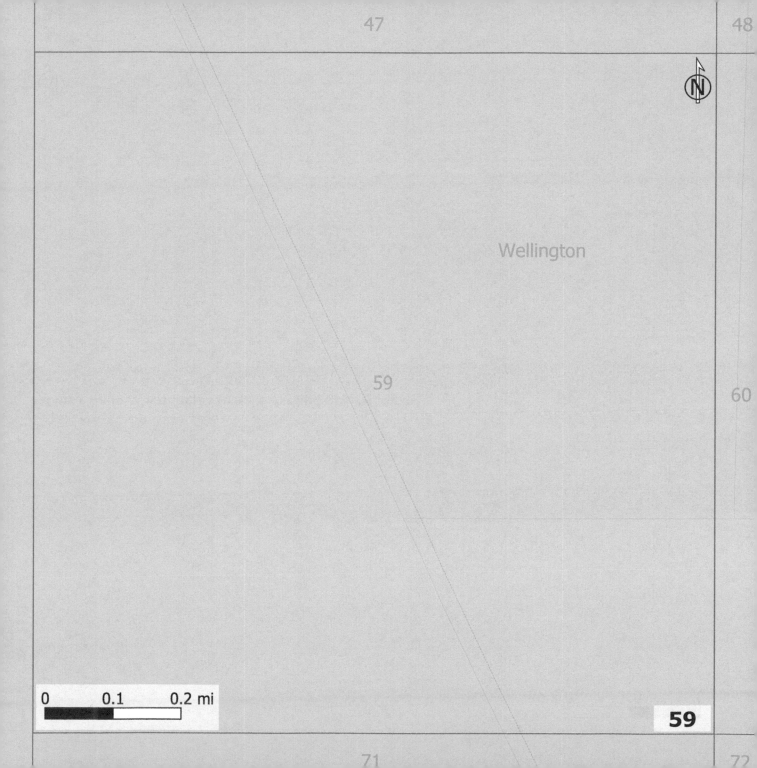

N

Wellington

59

0   0.1   0.2 mi

59

60

Arthur R. Marshall Loxahatchee National Wildlife Refuge

Wellington

0   0.1   0.2 mi

60

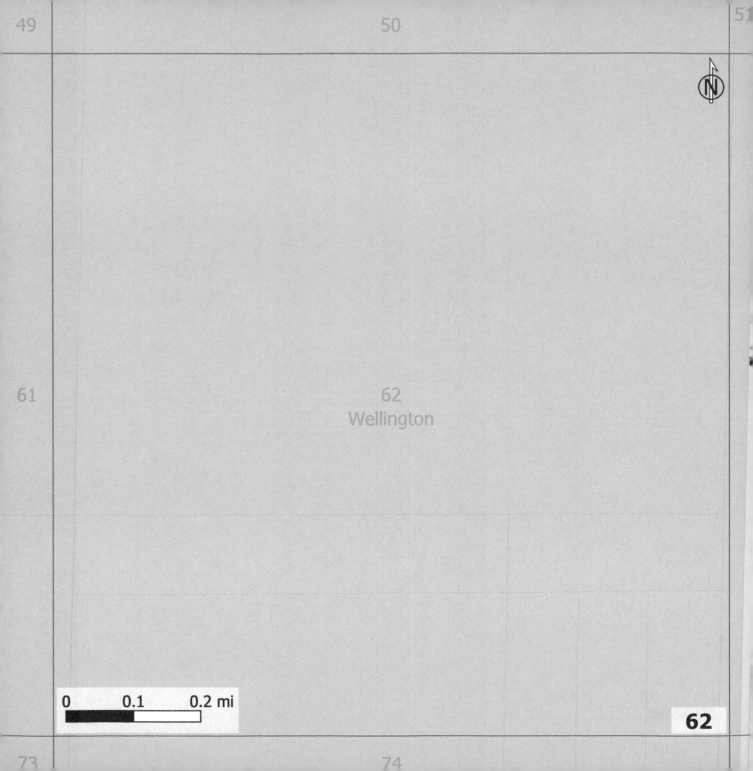

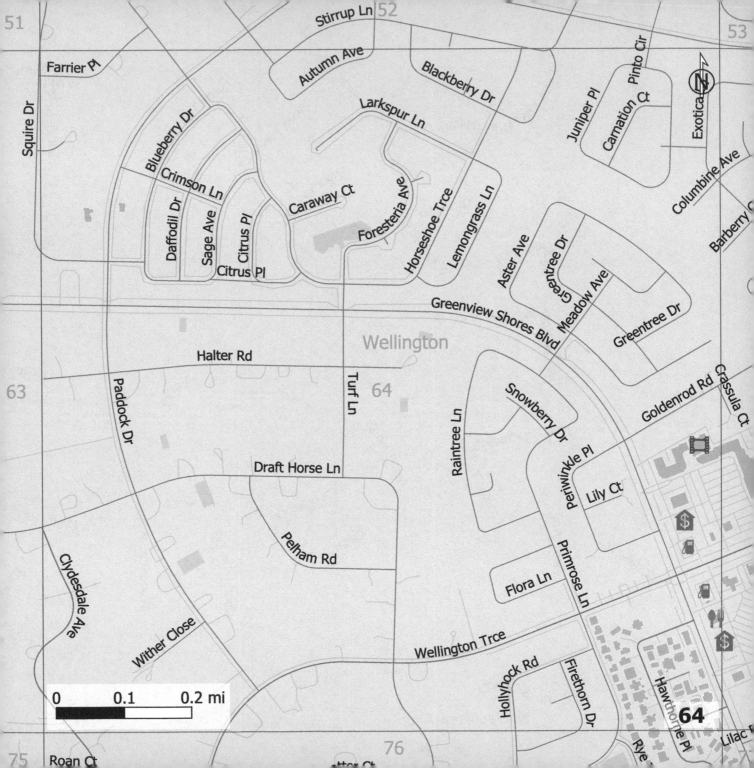

51
52
53

Stirrup Ln

Farrier Pl

Autumn Ave

Blackberry Dr

Juniper Pl

Pinto Cir

Carnation Ct

Exotica

N

Squire Dr

Blueberry Dr

Larkspur Ln

Crimson Ln

Columbine Ave

Daffodil Dr

Sage Ave

Citrus Pl

Caraway Ct

Foresteria Ave

Horseshoe Trce

Lemongrass Ln

Barberry

Citrus Pl

Aster Ave

Greentree Dr

Meadow Ave

Greentree Dr

Greenview Shores Blvd

Wellington

Halter Rd

Turf Ln

63

64

Paddock Dr

Raintree Ln

Snowberry Dr

Goldenrod Rd

Crassula Ct

Periwinkle Pl

Lily Ct

Draft Horse Ln

Pelham Rd

Flora Ln

Primrose Ln

Clydesdale Ave

Wither Close

Wellington Trce

Hollyhock Rd

Firethorn Dr

Hawthorne Pl

Lilac

0   0.1   0.2 mi

64

75

Roan Ct

76

tter Ct

Rye

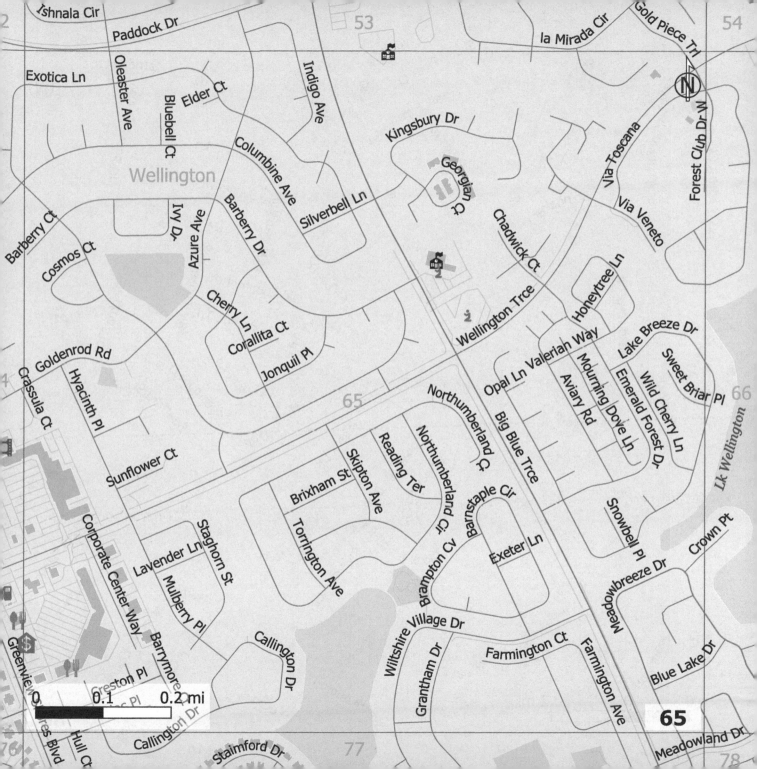

Shoma Dr

Shoma Dr

Shoma Dr

Shoma Dr

Shoma Dr

Shoma Dr

Shoma Dr

Shoma Dr

Pioneer R

Kensington Way

Royal Palm Beach

Berenger Walk

Victoria Grove Bend

Newberry Ln

Lancaster Way

Hamilton Ter

Christina Dr

101st Trl S

Canterbury Pl

State Hwy 7

Canyon Way

Keystone Ct

Bay View Way

Fishpond Ct

Falls St

Canyon Way

68

Creekside Dr

Old Hammock Way

Wellington

Range Line Rd

Beacon Cir

Galleria St

Galleria

Marsh St

US Hwy 441

Stonehaven Estates Dr

Beacon Cir

Beacon Cir

Beacon Cir

0   0.1   0.2 mi

Oak Bend Way

68

Oak Bend Way

Carriage Brooke Dr

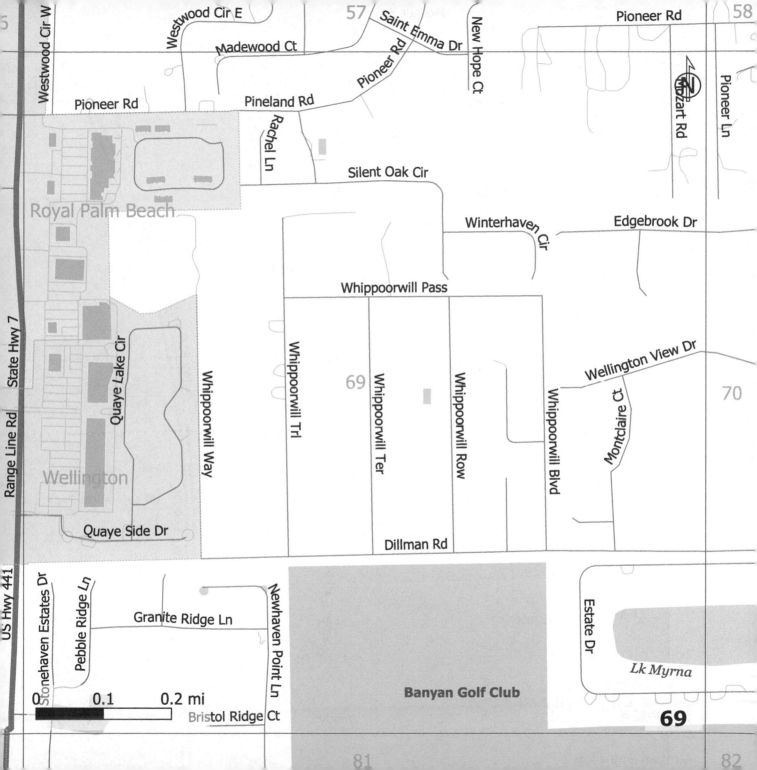

Wellingto

N

83

71

Arthur R. Marshall Loxahatchee National Wildlife Refuge

72

0   0.1   0.2 mi

71

83

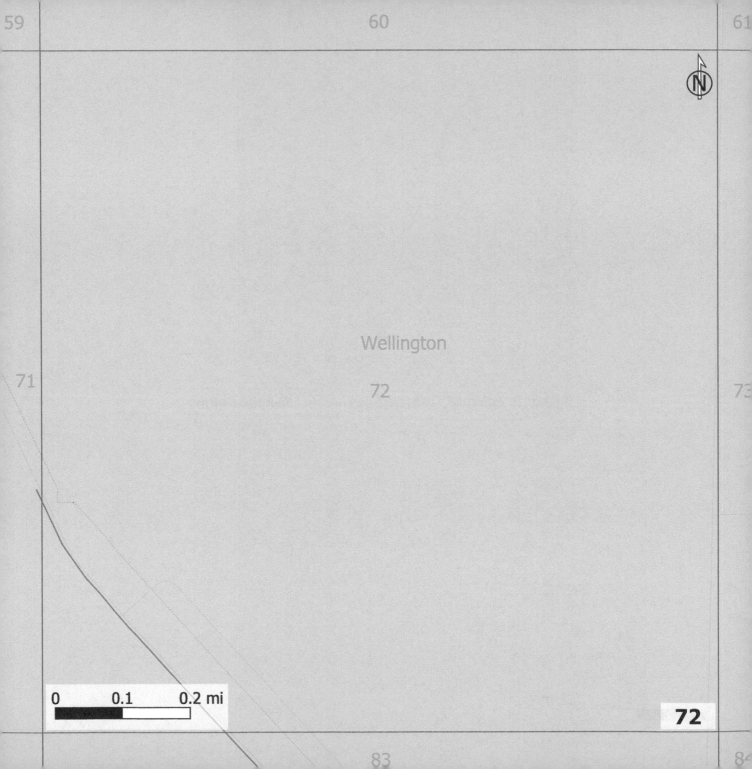

73
Wellington

74

0   0.1   0.2 mi

73

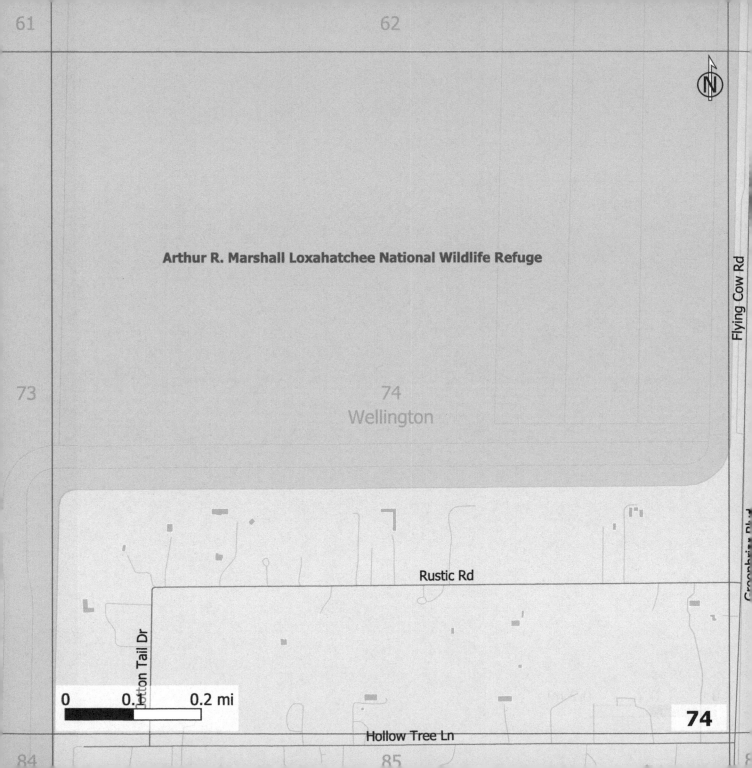

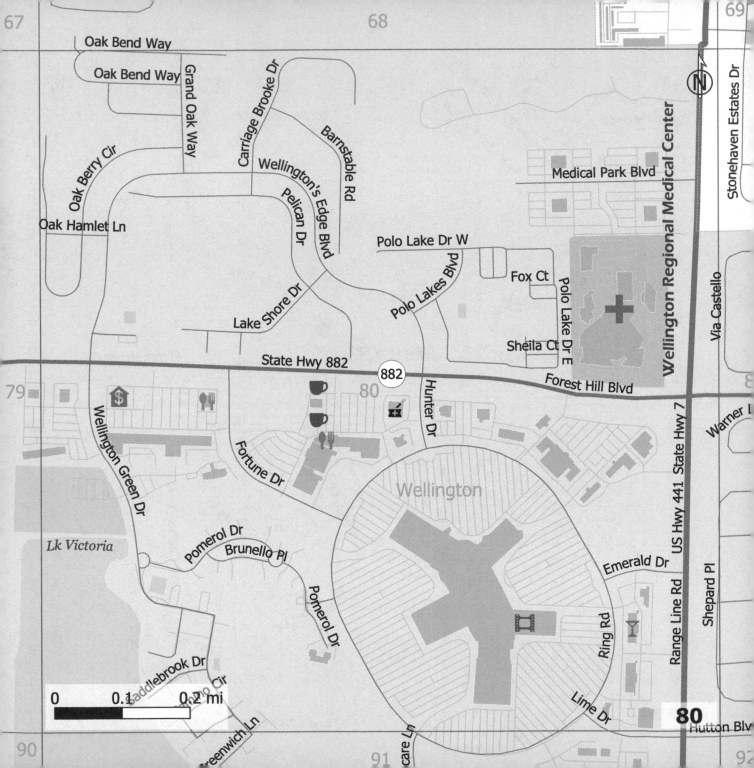

Bristol Ridge Ct

69

70

Coventry Lake Ct

Banyan Golf Club

N

Stonehaven Estates Dr

Royal Cardigan Way

Newhaven Point Ln

Via Elegante

Via Brilliante

Via Fiore

Via Castello

Via Classico E

Via Prestigo W

Via Prima

Via Allegro

Via Grande W

Via Buena Vida

Via Grande E

State Hwy 882

81

882

Forest Hill Blvd

82

Warner Ln

Wolcott Pl

Woodworth Ct

Wyeth Ct

Fatio Blvd

Olympia Blvd

Alworth Ter

Worswick Ct

Alexandra Cir

Wellington

Widener Ter

Stotesbury Way

Merriweather Way

Shearson Blvd

Dupont Pl

Waburton Ter

0   0.1   0.2 mi

Shepard Pl

Hutton Blvd

81

Cooper Way

92

93

30

69

70

Wendy Ln E

Wendy Ln W

Banyan Golf Club

Lk Banyan

Wendy Ln S

Via Brilliante

Via Prima

Via Prestigo E

Via Bellezza

Via Grande E

State Hwy 882 Forest Hill Blvd

81

82 Villagewalk Cir

Futana Way

Lyons Rd

Alworth Ter

Biddle Ct

Balsan Way

Eleuthera Ln

Alexandra Cir

Wellington

Inagua Ln

Dominica Pl

Jolly Harbour Ct

Cozumel Ln

Kaliko Ln

Shearson Blvd

Dupont Pl

Belize Pl

Laborie Ln

0   0.1   0.2 mi

Arima Ln

Montse

92

State Hwy 91 Florida's Tpke   Florida's Tpke

Okeeheelee Park

N

882

State Hwy 91

Okeeheelee Park S

82

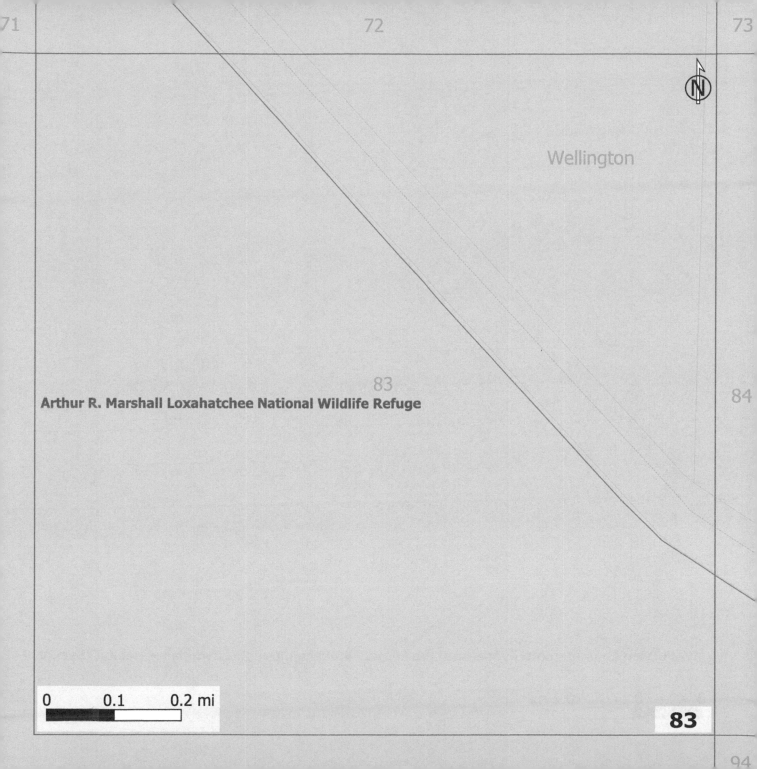

72

Wellington

83

84

Arthur R. Marshall Loxahatchee National Wildlife Refuge

0   0.1   0.2 mi

94

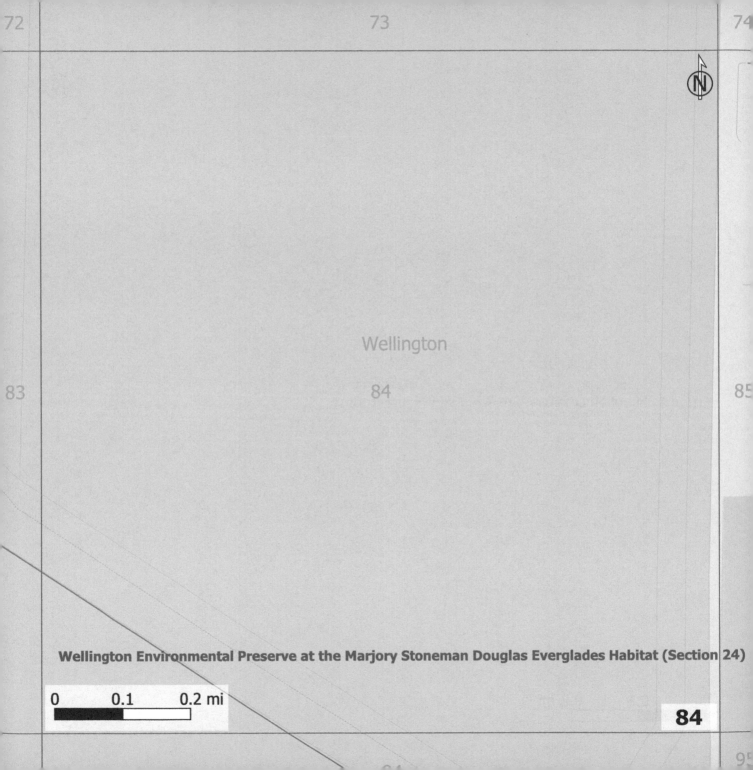

72

73

74

N

Wellington

83

84

85

Wellington Environmental Preserve at the Marjory Stoneman Douglas Everglades Habitat (Section 24)

0   0.1   0.2 mi

84

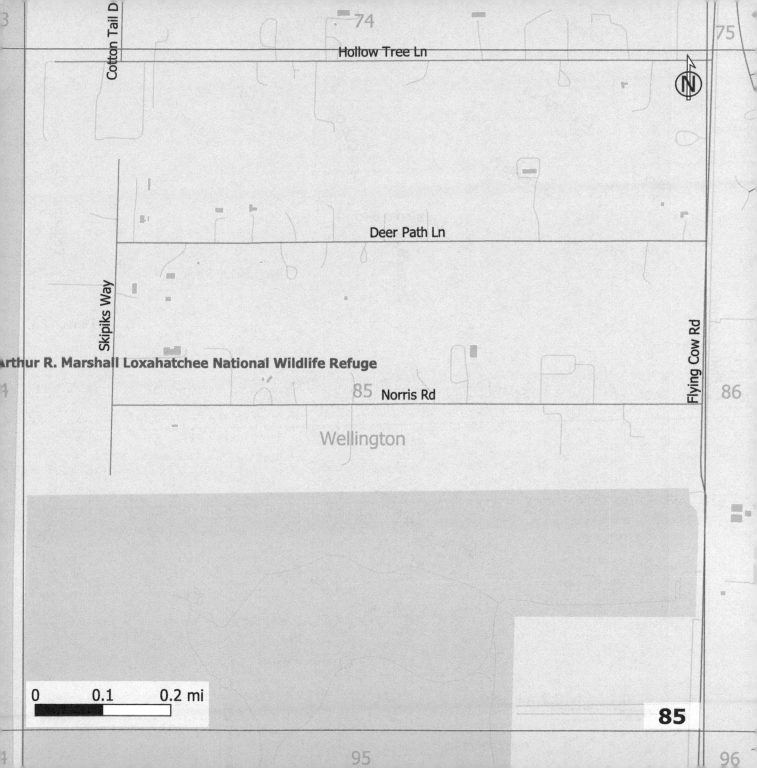

Cotton Tail D

73

74

75

Hollow Tree Ln

N

Deer Path Ln

Skipiks Way

Arthur R. Marshall Loxahatchee National Wildlife Refuge

85   Norris Rd

86

Flying Cow Rd

Wellington

0   0.1   0.2 mi

85

95

96

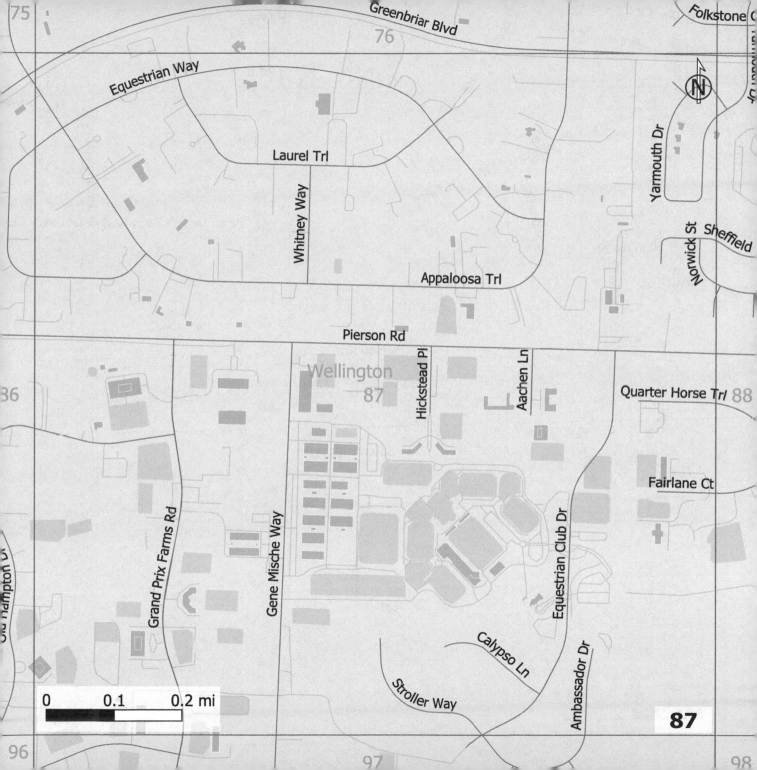

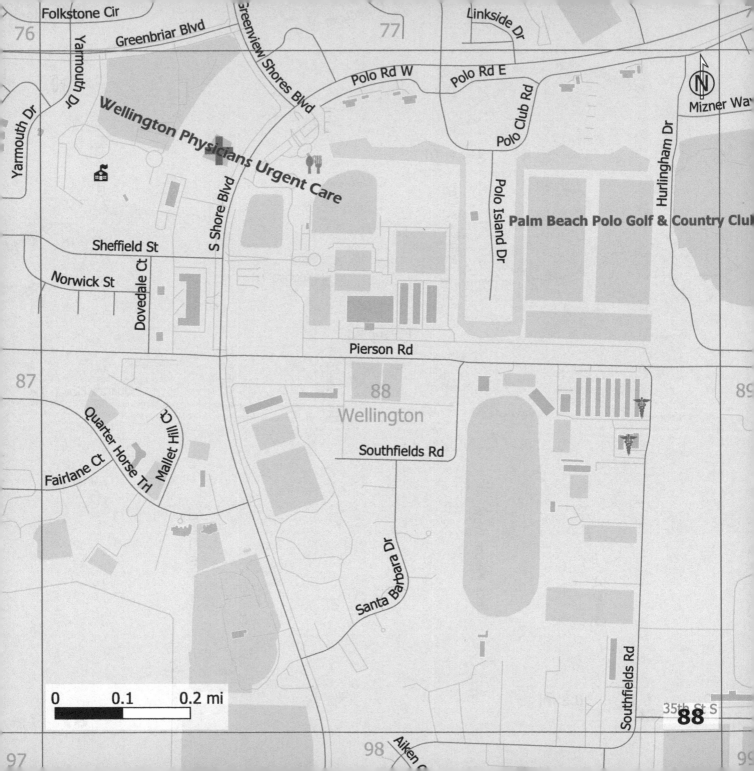

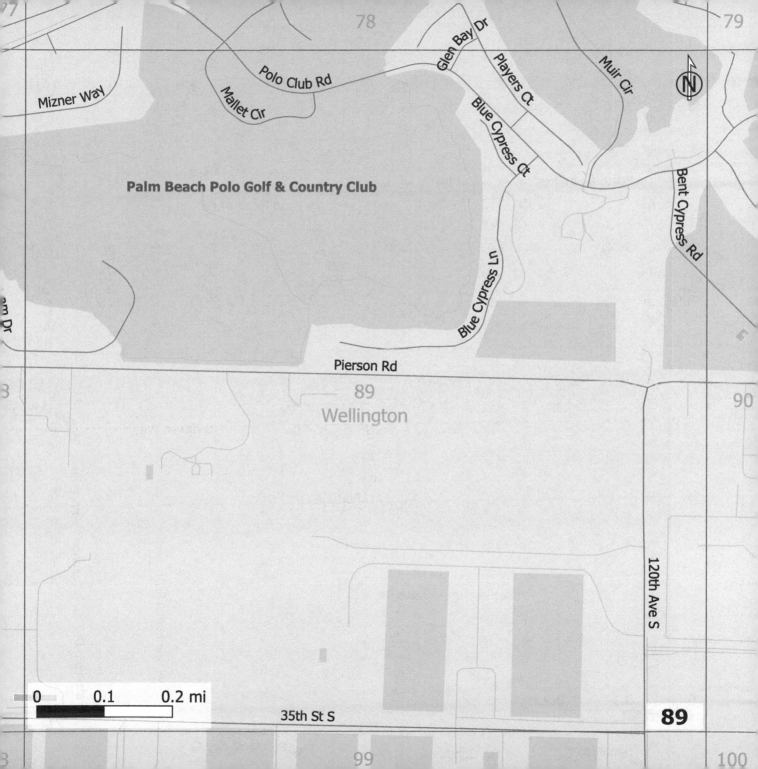

Mizner Way

Polo Club Rd

Mallet Cir

Glen Bay Dr

Players Ct

Muir Cir

Blue Cypress Ct

Bent Cypress Rd

Palm Beach Polo Golf & Country Club

Blue Cypress Ln

Pierson Rd

89

Wellington

90

120th Ave S

0   0.1   0.2 mi

35th St S

89

99

100

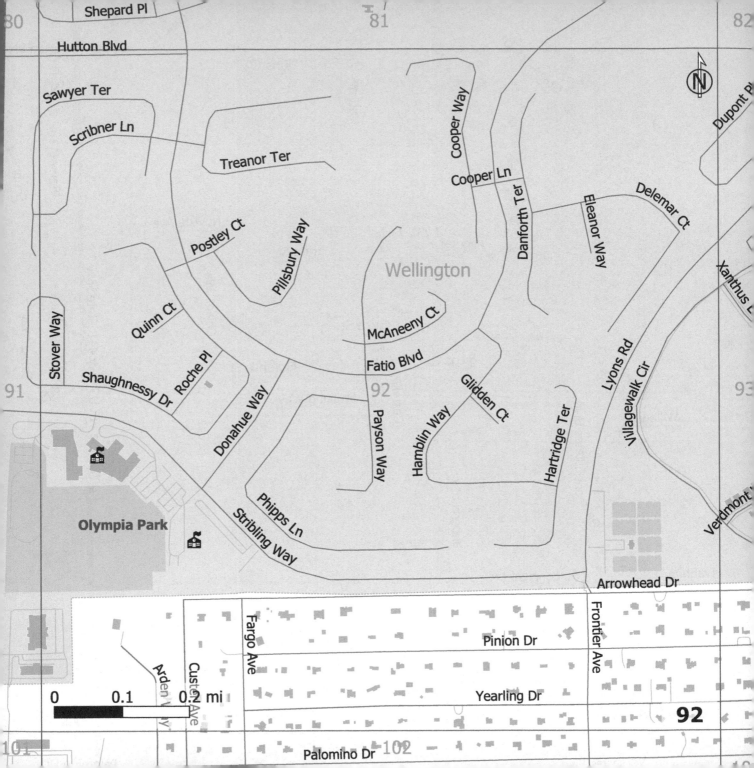

Shepard Pl

80   81   82

Hutton Blvd

N

Sawyer Ter

Scribner Ln

Treanor Ter

Cooper Way

Cooper Ln

Dupont Pl

Danforth Ter

Delemar Ct

Postley Ct

Pillsbury Way

Wellington

Eleanor Way

Xanthus L

Stover Way

Quinn Ct

McAneeny Ct

Fatio Blvd

91   92   93

Shaughnessy Dr

Roche Pl

Donahue Way

Payson Way

Hamblin Way

Glidden Ct

Lyons Rd

Villagewalk Cir

Hartridge Ter

Olympia Park

Phipps Ln

Stribling Way

Verdmont

Arrowhead Dr

Fargo Ave

Pinion Dr

Frontier Ave

Arden Way

Custer Ave

0   0.1   0.2 mi

Yearling Dr

92

101   Palomino Dr   102

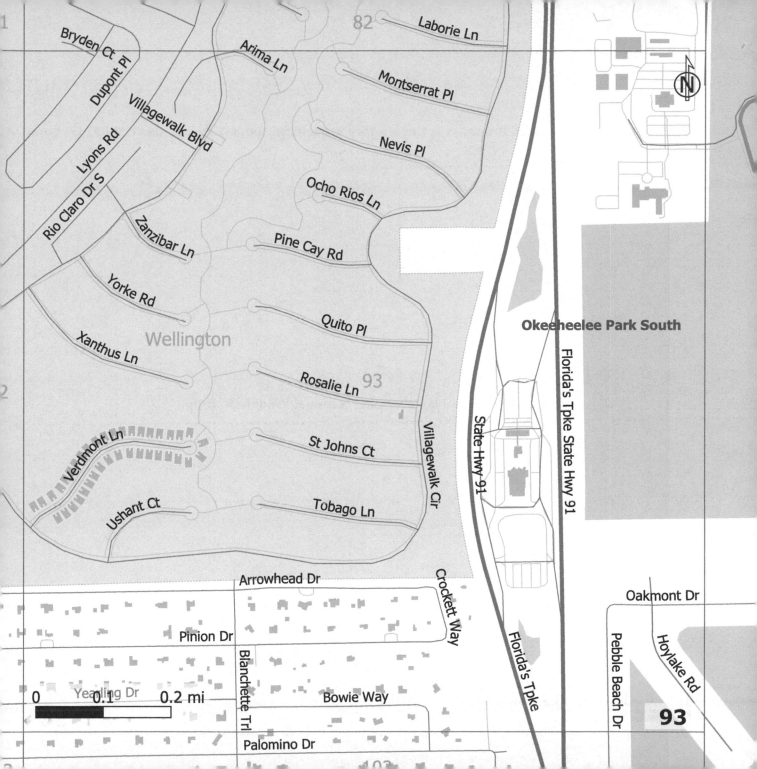

N

Wellington Environmental Preserve at the Marjory Stoneman Douglas Everglades Habitat (Section 24)

94

Arthur R. Marshall Loxahatchee National Wildlife Refuge

| 0 | 0.1 | 0.2 mi |

84

85

86

Loxahatchee Airport

Wellington

Flying Cow Rd

94

95

96

Arthur R. Marshall Loxahatchee National Wildlife Refuge

| 0 | 0.1 | 0.2 mi |

95

104

Ocean Breeze Ln

Hampton

Sunnyland Ln

Shutterfly Way

40th St S

Flying Cow Rd

Palma Ln

96

Wellington

Estancia Ln

Palm Beach Point Blvd

Sunset Ln

Palm Breeze Trl

Garden Point Trl

0   0.1   0.2 mi

46th Ln S

Indian Mound

10

87

35th St S

Southfields Rd

Aiken Ct

Middleburg Dr

Field 11

Fieldview Way

Via Christina

Lake Worth Rd

Gracida St

40th St S

S Shore Blvd

97

98
Wellington

130th Ave S

128th Ter S

0   0.1   0.2 mi

Indian Mound Rd

98

105

106

Paso Fino Dr

Miramontes Cir

Old Lighthouse Cir

Narragansett Bay Ct

Alameda Bay Ct

Moon Bay Ct

Nantucket Bay Ct

Versailles Blvd

Arcole Ct

Mabillon Way

Lake Isles Dr

Waterbend Ct

Isles Way S

Isles View Dr

Edgewater Cir

Grandview Mnr

Northgreen Dr

99   100 Lake Worth Rd

Wellington

Bahia Isle Cir

Isles Blvd

Bluff Harbor Way

Laurel Walk Rd

Pacifica St

Bahia Isle Cir

Isles Vista Blvd

Sea Mist Way

Stone Creek St

Osprey Pointe Cir

S Sea Ct

Mariners Cove Dr

Wellington Shores Dr

Silver Ridge St

Imperial Club Ln

Wycliffe Golf & Country Club

Island Reef Dr

Nautica Ct

100

Cobblefield Rd

Hazleton Ln

0   0.1   0.2 mi

107   Sunrise View Ln   108   Marina Bay Rd

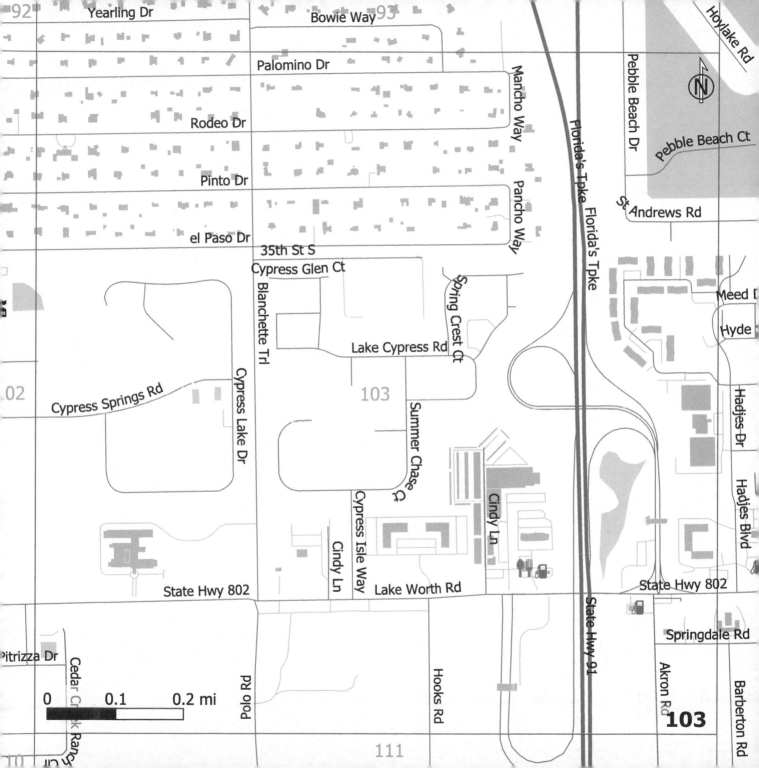

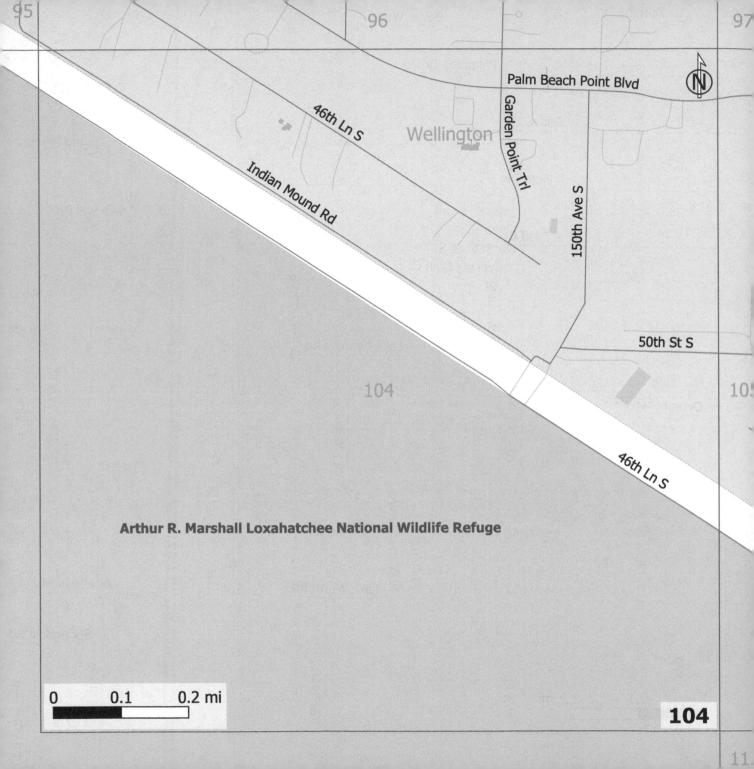

95

96

97

Palm Beach Point Blvd

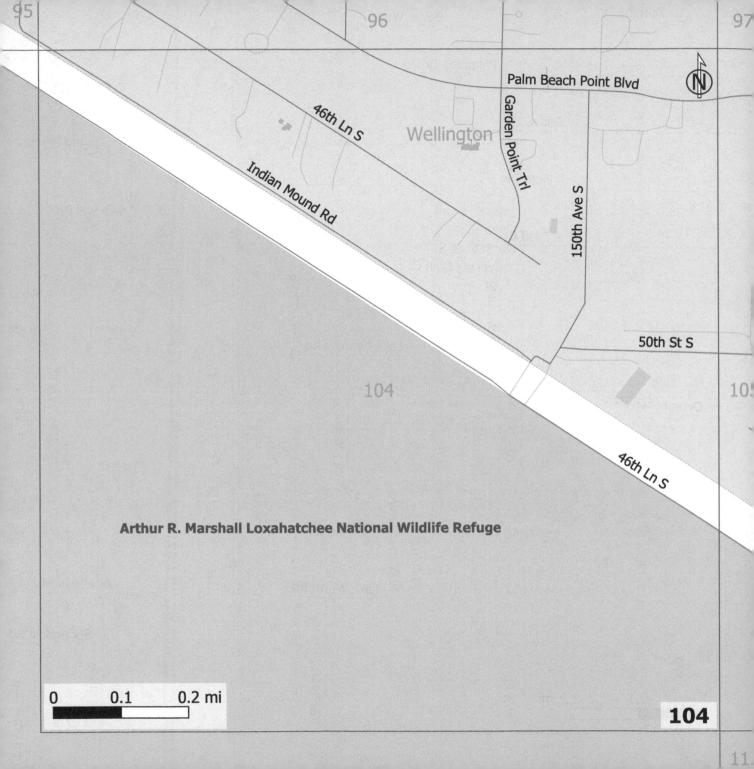N

46th Ln S

Wellington

Garden Point Trl

Indian Mound Rd

150th Ave S

50th St S

105

104

46th Ln S

11

Arthur R. Marshall Loxahatchee National Wildlife Refuge

0   0.1   0.2 mi

104

Palm Beach Point Blvd

South Rd

Stables Way

140th Ave S

50th St S

Wellington

105

106

Saddle Club Way

Hunter Ln

Jumper Rd

Las Palmas Ave

140th Ave S

138th Trl S

46th Ln S

53rd Rd S

55th St S

Arthur R. Marshall Loxahatchee National Wildlife Refuge

0   0.1   0.2 mi

97

98

9

N

Pelham Cir

Pelham Cir

50th St S

105

106

1

Wellington

S Shore Blvd

130th Ave S

52nd Pl S

Wellington Preserve Blvd

53rd Rd S

0   0.1   0.2 mi

55th St S

106

112

113

1

98

100

Indian Mound Rd

Windward Cove N

S 125th Ave

Isles Vista Blvd

120th Ave S

06

50th St S   107   108

Wellington

Everglades Way

Wellington Preserve Blvd

Hawk Hollow

Laredo Way

Lasso Way

Duckweed Rd

Otter Run

107

| 0 | 0.1 | 0.2 mi |

13

114

115

Nautica Ct

Cobblefield Rd

Sunrise View Ln

Windward Cove Ln

Marina Bay Rd

Paradise Cove Ln

Island Reef Dr

Isles Vista Blvd

Mariners Cove Dr

Maritime Ct

Manderly Ln

Wellington

Wycliffe Golf & Country Club

Manatee Bay Ln

Manderly Dr

Knightsbridge Pl

Regatta Ln

Windsor Bay Pl

Mainsail Ct

50th St S

Hawk Hollow

Tamis

Cougars Prowl

Homeland Rd

Michlar Dr

Otter Run

Pinelands Cir

Ira Ln

Anderson L

Cattail Ci

Reynolds Rd

0   0.1   0.2 mi

108

55th St S

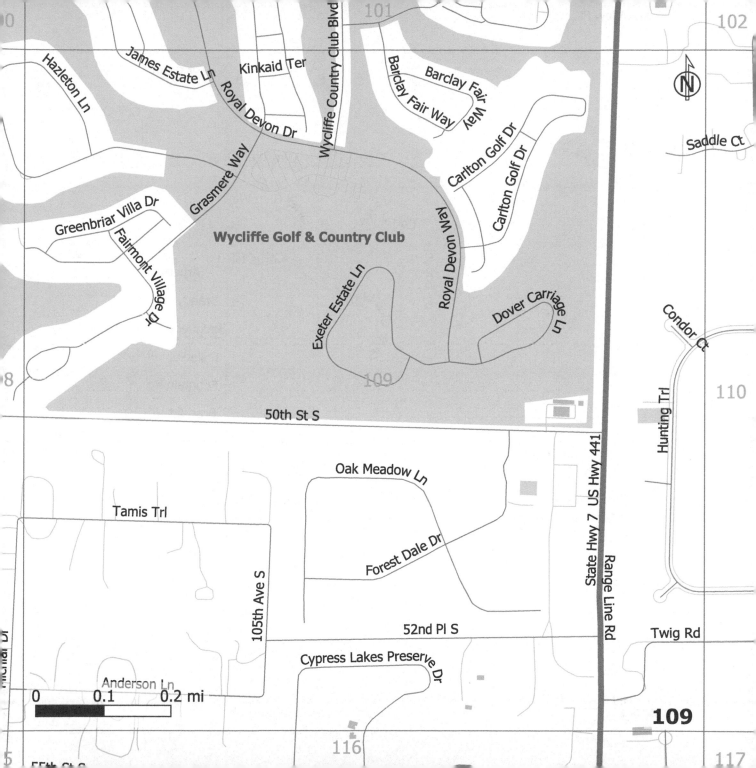

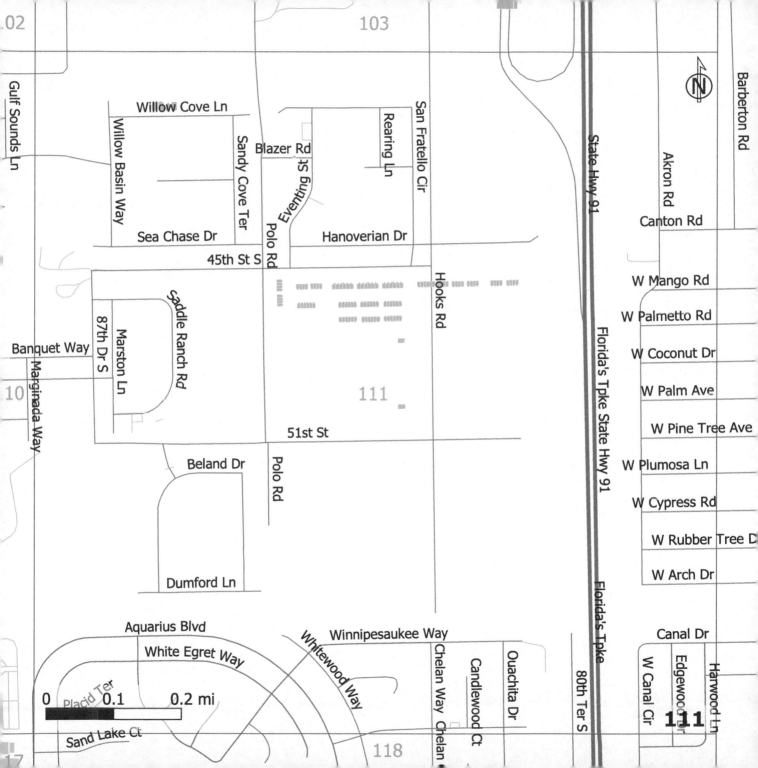

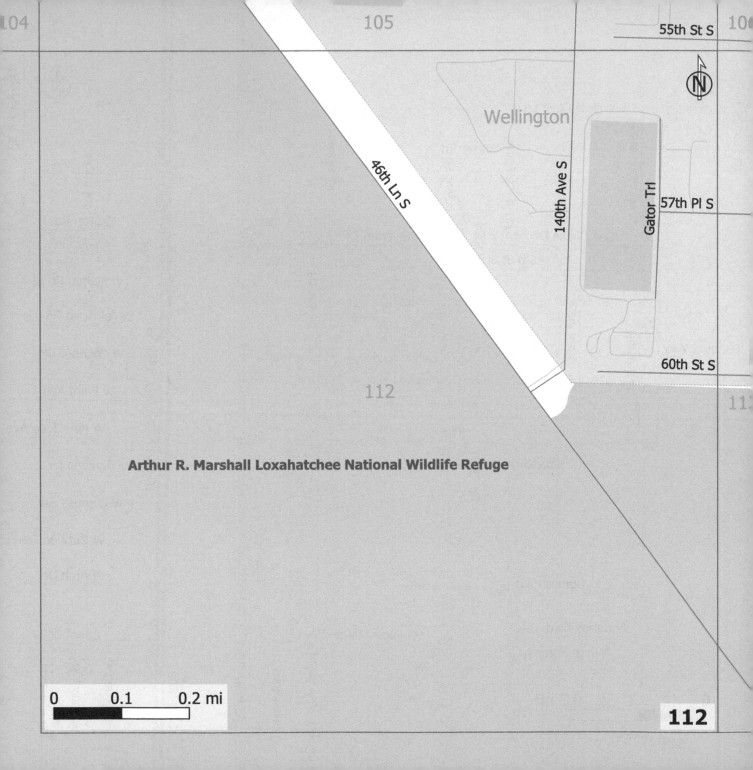

105

55th St S

N

Wellington

46th Ln S

140th Ave S

Gator Trl

57th Pl S

60th St S

11

112

Arthur R. Marshall Loxahatchee National Wildlife Refuge

0   0.1   0.2 mi

112

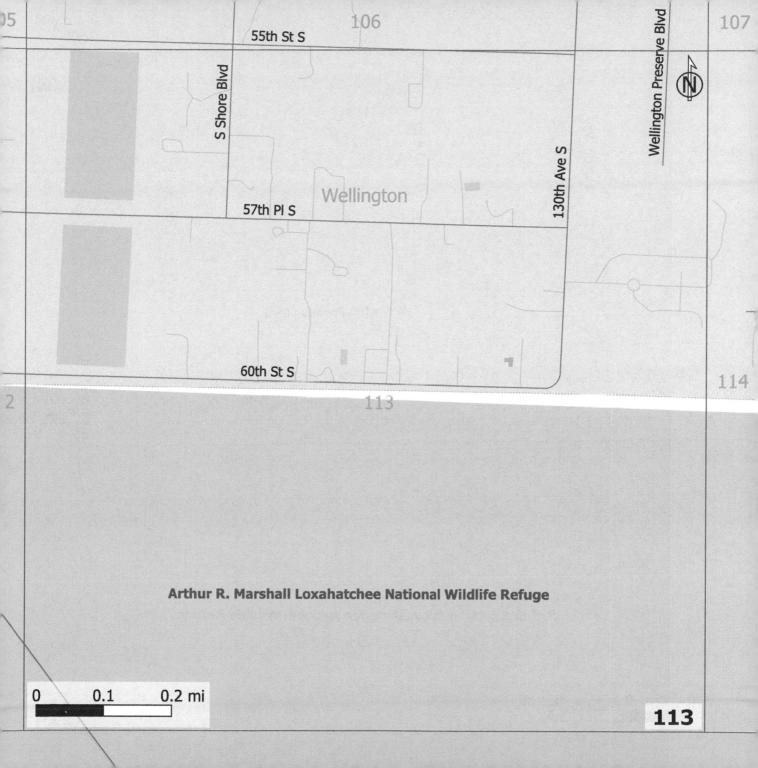

55th St S

S Shore Blvd

Wellington Preserve Blvd

130th Ave S

Wellington

57th Pl S

60th St S

N

Arthur R. Marshall Loxahatchee National Wildlife Refuge

0   0.1   0.2 mi

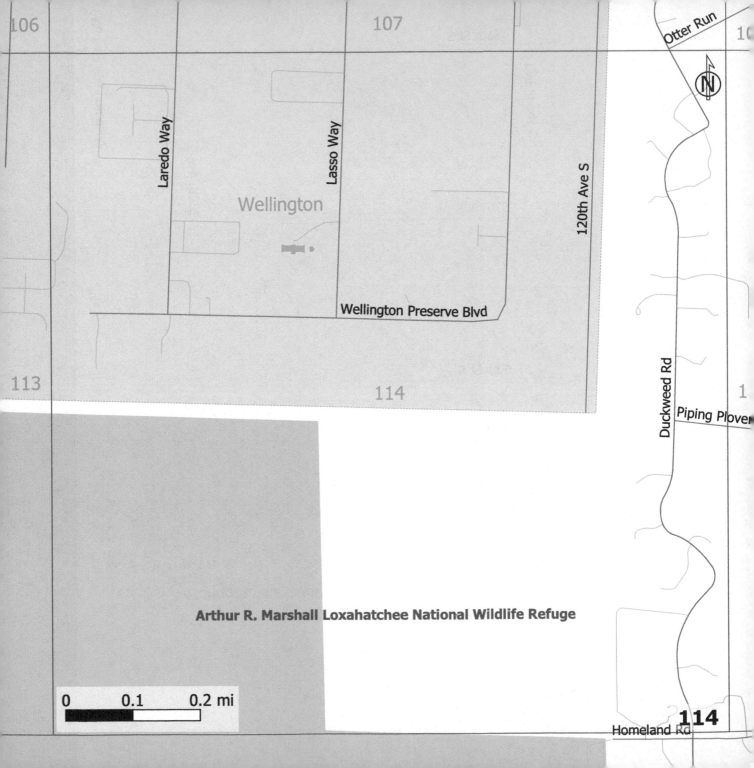

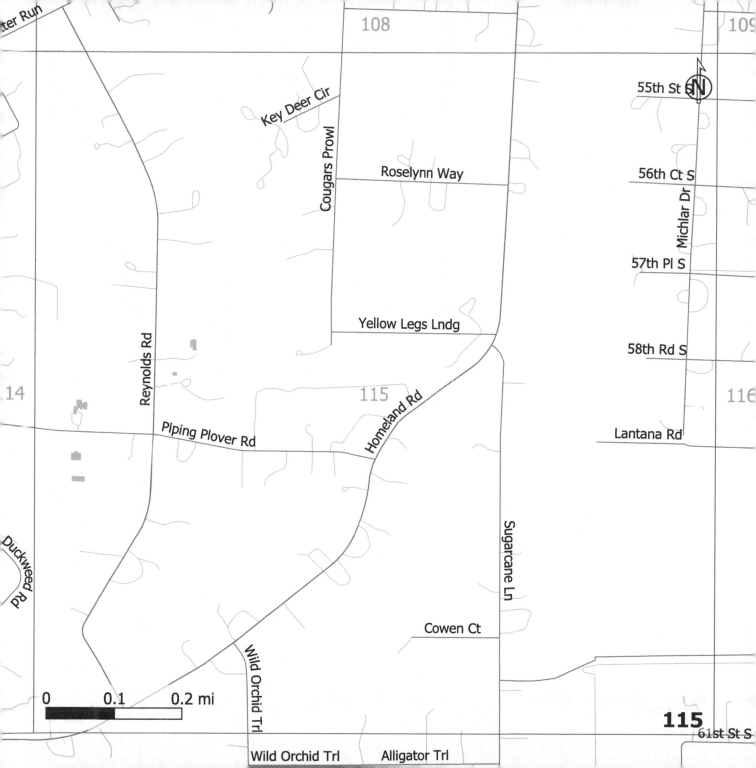

Marsh Wren Ct

Herons Nest Ct.

Woodwind Ln

White Egret Way

Park Ridge Golf Course

95th Ave S

Aquarius Blvd

White Sands Cv

Grassy Isle Trl

Lakepoint Ct

117

Lyons Rd

State Hwy 812 Lantana Rd

Mantova Dr

Positano Way

Pineville Dr

Quarry Rd Bellaggio Lakes Blvd

Torino Dr

Walnut Hill Dr

Oak Alley Dr

Taormina St

Kelty St

60th Ter S

Via Prim

0   0.1   0.2 mi

Argento

Bergamo St

us Rd

Perth Rd

117

gnello St

tona St

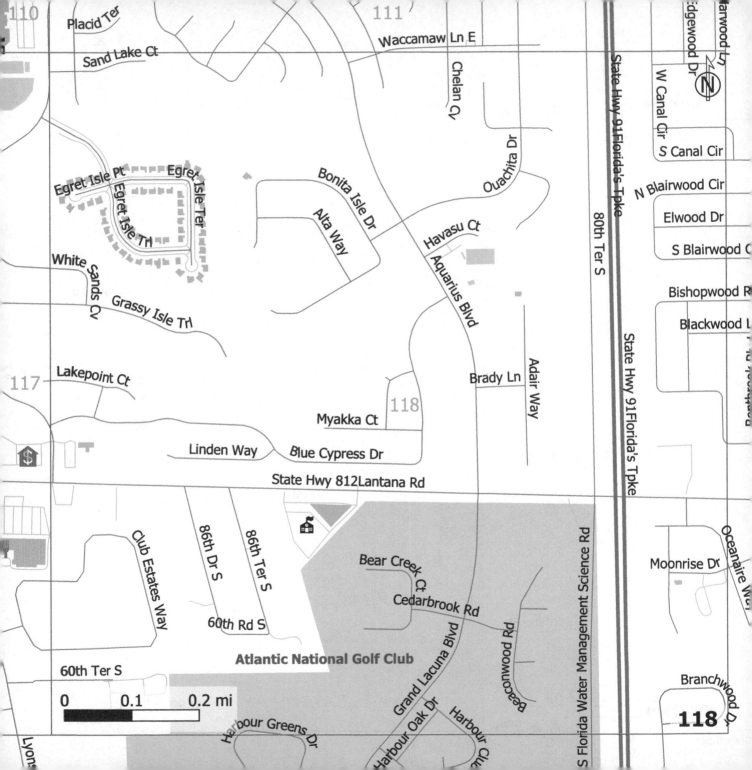

INDEX

101st Trl S, 68
103rd Ave N, 56
105th Ave N, 56
105th Ave S, 109
106th Ave S, 56
10th Pl N, 39
110th Ave N, 10
11th Ln N, 41
11th Ter, 40
120th Ave N, 9
120th Ave S, 89, 99, 107, 114
121st Ter N, 9
122nd Dr N, 8
123rd Trl N, 8
126th Dr N, 8
127th Trl N, 8
128th Ter S, 99
129th Ave N, 8
12th Pl N, 41
130th Ave N, 8
130th Ave S, 98, 106, 113
130th Trl N, 8
131st St, 41
138th Trl S, 105
13th Pl N, 41, 42
140th Ave N, 7
140th Ave S, 97, 105, 112
147th Ave N, 6
147th Dr N, 28
148th Ter N, 6
149th Ave N, 52
14th Pl N, 41
150th Ave S, 86, 104
152nd St N, 5
15th St N, 46
160th St N, 5

161st Ter N, 5, 15
168th Ter, 4, 14, 26, 38
168th Trl N, 4, 14, 26, 38
17th Rd N, 27, 28
17th St N, 30
180th St, 3, 13
185th Trl N, 2, 12
1st Ln S, 58
200th Trl N, 1
21st St N, 28
22nd Ct N, 30
22nd Rd N, 28, 29
23rd Ct N, 29
24th Cir N, 28
24th Ct N, 28, 29
25th Pl N, 27, 28
25th St N, 30
27th Ln N, 16
28th Ln N, 15, 16
30th Ct, 16
30th Ln N, 13, 14
31st Rd N, 13, 14
32nd Ln N, 13, 14
33rd Rd N, 13, 14
34th Pl N, 16
35th Pl N, 3, 13, 14, 17
35th St, 102
35th St S, 88, 89, 99, 103
36th Ct N, 3, 4
37th Pl N, 3, 4
38th Ln N, 3, 4
38th Rd N, 3, 4
3rd Pl S, 70
40th Ln N, 7, 8
40th Run N, 2, 3, 4
40th St N, 5, 6, 7, 8, 9, 10
40th St S, 96, 97, 98, 99
41st Ct N, 5, 9, 10
41st Ln N, 7, 8
41st Rd N, 2, 3, 4

42nd Rd N, 2, 3, 4, 5, 7, 8, 9, 10
42nd St N, 5
42nd Trl, 40
43rd Rd N, 2, 3, 4, 5, 6, 7, 8
44th Pl N, 2, 3, 4, 7, 8
44th St N, 5
45th St S, 111
46th Ct N, 7, 8
46th Ln S, 96, 104, 105, 112
46th Pl N, 9, 10
50th St S, 104, 105, 106, 107, 108, 109
51st St, 111
52nd Pl S, 106, 109
53rd Rd S, 105, 106
55th St S, 105, 106, 113, 115, 116
56th Ct S, 115, 116
57th Pl S, 112, 113, 115, 116
58th Rd S, 115, 116
5th St S, 70
60th Rd S, 118
60th St S, 112, 113
60th Ter S, 117, 118
6th Ct N, 40, 41, 42
7th Pl S, 70
80th Ter S, 111, 118
81st Ave, 70
82nd Dr S, 70
86th Dr S, 118
86th Ter S, 58, 70, 118
87th Dr S, 111
8th Pl N, 40
8th Rd N, 46
95th Ave N, 45, 57
95th Ave S, 110, 117
A Rd, 5, 15, 27, 39

Aachen Ln, 87
Acacia Ct, 42
Acme Rd, 55, 56, 57
Adair Way, 118
Adonider Ln, 65
Aero Club Dr, 63, 75, 86
Aiken Ct, 98
Aintree Dr E, 38
Aintree Dr W, 38
Akron Rd, 103, 111
Alamanda Ct, 54
Alameda Bay Ct, 100
Albright Ct, 65
Alcazar St, 19
Alder Ln, 66
Aldi Way, 32, 33
Aldsworth Ct, 77
Alexandra Cir, 81, 82
Alford Way, 77
Almeria St, 9
Alta Way, 118
Alworth Ter, 81
Amaryllis Ct, 65
Ambassador Dr, 87, 97
Amber Ct, 30
Amesbury Cir, 78
Amesbury Ct, 78
Amherst Ct, 19, 31
Andalusian Way, 91
Anderson Ln, 108, 109
Andover Coach Cir, 101
Andover Coach Ln, 101
Andros Isle, 34
Angelica Ct, 64
Angus Rd, 117
Anhinga Dr, 67
Annandale Cir, 30
Anniston Dr, 102
Anthony Groves Rd, 68
Appaloosa Trl, 75, 76, 86, 87

April Dr, 6
Aquarius Blvd, 110, 111, 117, 118
Aquarius Ln, 44
Arabian Dr, 25, 37
Arbor Ln, 18
Arborwood Way, 65
Arcadia Dr, 54, 66
Arcole Ct, 100, 101
Arden Lake Way, 35, 47
Arden Park Dr, 23, 35
Arden Way, 92, 102
Ardennes Way, 116
Areaca Dr, 54
Arima Ln, 93
Armadillo Way, 58
Arpege Pl, 110
Arrowhead Dr, 92, 93
Arrowhead Point Rd, 35
Arterra Ct, 32
Artist Pl, 110
Ashwood Ln, 111
Aster Ave, 64
Asturian Trl, 116
Athens Ter, 75
Atwell Dr, 58
Augustine Rd, 34
Autumn Ave, 64
Aviary Rd, 65
Avocado Blvd, 7
Azalea Dr, 43, 55
Azure Ave, 53, 65
Azure Ct, 65
B Rd, 5, 15, 27, 39, 51
Bahia Isle Cir, 100
Bald Eagle Ct, 30
Balfour Point Dr, 34
Balsam Dr, 55
Balsan Way, 82
Baltrusol Pl, 79
Bama Ln, 58

Banbury Way, 75
Banquet Way, 110, 111
Banyan Ln, 31
Barberry Ct, 65
Barberry Dr, 65
Barcelona Dr, 31
Barclay Fair Way, 101, 109
Barnstable Rd, 80
Barnstaple Cir, 65
Barnstormer Ct, 75
Barrington Woods Dr, 65
Barrymore Ct, 65
Basin St, 78
Basin St E, 78
Basin St N, 78
Basin St S, 78
Basin St W, 78
Basswood Pl, 66
Bauer Rd, 8, 18
Bay Breeze Ct, 100
Bay Cedar Ct, 43
Bay Harbour Cir, 33, 34
Bay Point Cir, 33, 34
Bay View Way, 68
Baybury Ln, 46
Bayridge Pl, 78
Baywinds Dr, 33
Beacon Cir, 68
Beacon Pointe Ln, 100
Beaconwood Rd, 118
Bear Creek Ct, 118
Bearing Pt, 34
Beaver Dam Ct, 30
Bedford Ct, 19
Bedford Ln, 77
Bedford Mews Ct, 77
Bedford Mews Dr, 77, 88
Beland Dr, 111
Belcara Ct, 32

Belhaven Ct, 65
Belize Pl, 82
Bella Terra Way, 44, 45
Bella Vista Ct S, 44
Bella Vista Dr, 31
Bella Vista Way, 44, 56
Bellaggio Lakes Blvd, 117
Bellanca Ln, 75
Bellarosa Cir, 20, 21, 32, 33
Bellcrest Cir, 18, 19
Bellcrest Ct, 18, 19
Belle Grove Ln, 57, 58
Belleek Dr, 46
Bellezza Ter, 44
Bellhurst Way, 45, 46
Belmont Dr, 19
Belmont Trce, 75, 76
Belmore Ct, 67
Belmore Ter, 67
Belvedere Rd, 44, 45, 46
Benoist Farms Rd, 34, 46, 58
Benoist Farms Rd S, 58
Bent Creek Rd, 51
Bent Cypress Rd, 89, 90
Bent Oak, 31
Bent Pine Cir E, 102
Bent Pine Cir W, 102
Berenger Walk, 68
Berrywood Dr, 118
Biddix Rd, 28, 29
Biddle Ct, 82
Big Blue Trce, 53, 65, 77, 78
Big Blue Trl, 78
Big Cone Ct, 66
Big Wood Cay, 34
Bilbao St, 20, 31, 32
Binks Estate Dr, 51, 63
Binks Forest Dr, 51, 63

Binks Pointe Ter, 51
Birague Dr, 101
Birkdale Dr, 67, 79
Bishopwood Rd, 118
Black Birch Ct, 43
Black Falcon Rd, 11
Black Olive Cres, 42
Black Willow Ln, 67, 79
Blackberry Dr, 52, 64
Blackwood Ln, 118
Blanchette Trl, 93, 103
Blazer Rd, 111
Block Island Rd, 66
Blue Cypress Ct, 89
Blue Cypress Dr, 117, 118
Blue Cypress Ln, 89
Blue Diamond Pl, 65
Blue Lake Dr, 65, 66
Blue Swallow Ter, 65
Blue Violet Ln, 44
Bluebell Ct, 65
Blueberry Dr, 64
Bluff Harbor Way, 100
Bob Cat Ln, 23
Bobbie Ln, 44
Bobwhite Ct, 44
Bobwhite Rd, 32, 43, 44
Boeing Ct, 75, 86
Bolton Ct, 88
Bonanza Rd, 110
Bonita Isle Dr, 118
Bottlebrush Ct, 65
Bouquet Rd, 110
Bowie Way, 93, 103
Bowline Dr, 33
Bracelet Dr, 110
Brady Ln, 118
Braeburn Pl, 79
Brampton Cir, 65
Brampton Cv, 65

Branchwood Dr, 118
Branding Iron Ct, 66
Brandy Ln, 110
Brandywine Ct, 30
Breakers Pointe Way, 33
Breakers West Blvd, 33, 34, 45, 46
Breakers West Ct, 33
Breakers West Ter, 45
Breakers West Way, 45
Briar Oak Ct, 30
Briar Oak Dr, 30
Bridge Port Dr, 33
Brier Patch Ct, 79
Brier Patch Trl, 79
Brighton Dr E, 26
Brighton Dr W, 26
Brightstone St, 77
Brightwood Way, 66
Brinely Pl, 8, 18, 19
Brisbane Ln, 78
Bristol Ridge Ct, 69
Britten Ln, 75
Brixham St, 65
Broadleaf Ct, 66
Brook Woode Ave, 54, 55
Brunello Pl, 80
Bryan Rd, 29, 30
Bryden Ct, 82, 93
Buck Ridge Trl, 12, 24
Buckingham Ave, 65
Buckland Ct, 77, 78
Buckland Ct E, 78
Buckland St, 78
Burlington Ct, 118
Burlwood Ln, 118
Burns Dr E, 38
Burns Dr W, 38
Burton Ter, 77
Business Pkwy, 44, 45

Butler Greenwood Dr, 58
Button Bush Ln, 51
C Rd, 6, 16, 28, 40, 51, 52
Cabbage Palm Way, 2, 12
Cabot Ln, 78
Cactus Hill Ct, 30
Cadiz St, 19, 20
Calamint Pt, 44, 56
Calamondin Blvd, 2
Calder Dr E, 38
Calder Dr W, 38
Calida Dr, 34
Callington Dr, 65, 77
Calypso Ln, 87
Cambridge Ln, 30, 42
Camellia Dr, 43, 55
Camelot Ct, 42
Camino Cir, 80, 91
Canal Dr, 111
Canal Rd, 1
Canalily Way, 65
Candlenut Ct, 43
Candlewood Ct, 111
Cane Field Trce, 35, 47
Canosa Ct, 63
Canter Way, 76
Canterbury Cir, 79
Canterbury Pl, 68
Canton Rd, 111
Canyon Way, 68
Cape Ivy Pt, 43, 44
Capeside Cir, 78
Caraway Ct, 64
Cargill Pt, 34
Carissa Dr, 43, 55
Carlton Golf Dr, 109
Carlton St, 77
Carmen Ln, 44

Carnation Ct, 64
Carousel Way, 44
Carrera Ln, 75
Carriage Brooke Dr, 80
Carriage Ln, 66
Cascade Falls Cir, 102
Casey Rd, 41, 42
Casey Wilson Rd, 41
Castaway Ct, 36
Castellina Way, 91
Castillo St, 32
Castlebridge Rd, 69
Catania Way, 44
Cattail Cir, 108
Cayo Costa Ct, 43
Cazadero Ct, 20
Cedar Bluff Pl, 63
Cedar Cove Rd, 63
Cedar Creek Ranch Cir, 102, 103, 110, 111
Cedar Grove Ln, 63
Cedarbrook Rd, 118
Cessna Way, 86
Chadwick Ct, 65
Chancellor Dr, 78
Chandelle Pl, 86
Chappard Ct, 67
Chapparel Way, 67, 79
Charlee St, 102
Chatsworth Village Dr, 77
Chatuga Ct, 118
Cheetham Hill Blvd, 4, 14, 26, 38
Chelan Cv, 111, 118
Chelan Way, 111
Chelmsford St, 65
Cheltenham Dr E, 14
Cheltenham Dr W, 14
Cherry Ln, 65
Chesapeake Ct, 99, 100

Chestnut Cir, 42
Chestnut Ct, 18
Chianti Way, 91
Chickcharnies, 34
Chorus Way, 44, 45
Christina Dr, 68
Churchill Cir, 56
Churchill Dr, 18
Churchill Way, 18
Cindy Circle Ln, 67
Cindy Dr, 55, 67
Cindy Ln, 103
Citrus Dr, 52
Citrus Isle Ln, 110
Citrus Pl, 64
Civic Center Way, 31
Clinton Ct, 31
Clipper Cir, 21
Clipper Ct, 21, 33
Club Estates Way, 117, 118
Clubhouse Estates Ct, 33
Clubhouse Rd, 69
Clubhouse Turn Rd, 116
Clydesdale Ave, 63, 64, 76
Clydesdale Rd, 25, 37
Co Rd 700, 47, 48, 49, 50, 51, 52, 53, 54, 55, 56, 57, 58
Co Rd 882, 54, 66, 78
Coakley Pt, 34
Cobblefield Rd, 100
Coconut Blvd, 8
Cocoplum Cir, 42
Cocoplum Ln, 42
Cocoplum Sound Ln, 34
Cold Springs Ct, 66
Collecting Canal Rd, 39, 40, 41, 42
Collonade Dr, 101

Colony Dr, 43
Columbine Ave, 64, 65
Columbine Pl, 65
Compton Rd, 29, 30
Conaskonk Cir, 19
Concert Way, 44
Condor Ct, 109
Cool Oak Way, 118
Cooper Ln, 92
Cooper Way, 92
Copperpod Ct, 43
Copperwood Cir, 42
Coral Breeze Dr, 78
Corallita Ct, 65
Coralwood Ct, 67, 79
Corby Ct, 75
Cordoba Cir, 20, 32
Cordoda Cir, 20, 32
Cornflower Ct, 65
Cornwall Dr E, 26
Cornwall Dr W, 26
Corporate Center Way, 65
Corral Vw, 110
Corsica Dr, 63, 75
Cortes Ave, 20, 32
Cortile St, 20
Cortona St, 117
Cosmos Ct, 65
Cottagewood Ct, 57
Cottagewood Ln, 57, 69
Cotton Tail Dr, 74, 85
Cougars Prowl, 108, 115
Counrty Estates Dr, 117
Country Club Dr, 19, 31, 78
Country Club Way, 19, 31
Country Estates Dr, 117
Country Golf Dr, 75, 86
Country Vista Way, 103

Country Wood Ct, 66
Coventry Lake Ct, 81
Covington Ct, 118
Cowen Ct, 115
Cozumel Ln, 82
Cranberry Ct, 65
Cranes Roost, 31
Crape Myrtle Ln, 51
Crassula Ct, 64, 65
Creekside Dr, 68
Creston Pl, 65
Crestwood Blvd, 18, 19, 30, 42, 54
Crestwood Blvd N, 30, 42
Crestwood Cir, 42, 54
Crestwood Ct N, 54
Crestwood Ct S, 54
Crimson Ln, 64
Crockett Way, 93
Crocus Ct, 64
Cromer Ct, 77
Cross Breeze Dr, 78
Cross Pine Ct, 101, 102
Crossbill Ct, 109
Croton Dr, 43
Crowberry Ct, 52
Crown Pt, 65, 66
Cuddington Ct, 78
Cupids Cay, 22
Curley Cut, 34
Custer Ave, 92, 102
Cypress Chase Ln, 51
Cypress Creek Ln, 63
Cypress Cres, 42, 54
Cypress Edge Dr, 102
Cypress Glen Ct, 103
Cypress Green Cir, 51, 63
Cypress Grove Ln, 69
Cypress Island Ct, 78

Cypress Island Way, 78
Cypress Isle Way, 103
Cypress Key Way, 54
Cypress Lake Ave, 42, 54
Cypress Lake Dr, 103
Cypress Lakes Preserve Dr, 109, 116
Cypress Ln, 31
Cypress Park Dr, 63
Cypress Row Dr, 33, 34, 45
Cypress Springs Rd, 102, 103
Cypress Strand Ct, 51
Cypress Terrace Ct, 33
Cypress Trails Elem Dr, 42, 43
Cypress Trce, 42, 43, 54
Cypress Wood Ct, 102
Cypress Xing, 51, 63
D Rd, 6, 16, 28, 40, 52
Daffodil Dr, 64
Dahlia Dr, 55
Dalmany Way, 44
Danbury Ct, 31
Danforth Ter, 92
Daniella Dr, 102
Danielson Dr, 102, 110
Dartford Trl, 65
Dartmoor Dr, 78
de Havilland Ct, 75
Deer Creek Cir, 102
Deer Haven Dr, 35
Deer Path Ln, 85, 86
Deer Run Blvd, 23, 24, 25
Deer Run Trl, 11, 23
Deerfield Ct, 30
Deerwood Ct, 63, 64
Delemar Ct, 92
Dellwood Blvd, 2, 12

Denlow Ln, 44
Derby Dr E, 14
Derby Dr W, 4, 14
Derby Ln, 18, 19
Derby Trl, 79
Devonshire Cir, 68
Diamond Chip Ct, 100
Dickens Pl, 46
Dillman Rd, 69, 70
Doe Trl, 12, 24
Dogwood Ct, 54
Dollarspot Ct, 65
Dominica Pl, 82
Donahue Way, 92
Donlin Dr, 79
Donwoods Ln, 44
Dorchester Pl, 77
Doubletree Cir, 53
Doubletree Trl, 53
Dove Cir, 32, 44
Dovedale Ct, 88
Dover Carriage Ln, 109
Downers Dr E, 26
Downers Dr W, 26
Dracena Dr, 65
Draft Horse Ln, 63, 64, 75, 76
Dressage Ct, 80
Driggs Hill, 22
Drury Pl, 45
Duckweed Rd, 107, 114
Duellant Rd, 1
Dumford Ln, 111
Dunning Dr, 9, 19
Dunster Ct, 76
Dupont Pl, 81, 82, 92, 93
Duran Blvd E, 38
Duran Blvd W, 38
Durango Dr, 116
E Alan Black Blvd, 14
E Aquaduct Dr, 14

E Citrus Dr, 53
E Epsom Dr, 38
E Fairway Ter, 33
E Fontana Ct, 18
E Rambling Dr, 55, 67
E Rd, 7, 17, 29, 41, 53
E Wiltshire Dr, 26
Eagle Point Ln, 110
Earhart Pl, 75
East Ct, 43
Easthampton Cir, 66, 78
Eden Lake Ct, 111
Edgebrook Dr, 69, 70
Edgebrook Ln, 70
Edgefield Rd, 63
Edgewater Cir, 100
Edgewood Dr, 111, 118
Edinburgh Dr E, 14
Edinburgh Dr W, 14
Edith Rd, 41
Egret Chase Ln, 33
Egret Cove Dr, 33
Egret Isle Pt, 118
Egret Isle Ter, 118
Egret Isle Trl, 117, 118
Egret Ln, 23
Eider Ct, 32
el Paso Dr, 102, 103
Elder Ct, 65
Eleanor Way, 92
Elephant Walk, 25
Eleuthera Ln, 82
Elgin Ct, 76, 77
Elmbank Way, 44
Elmira Ct, 30
Elwood Dr, 118
Elysium Dr, 19
Ember Ridge Run, 35
Emerald Ct, 8
Emerald Dr, 80
Emerald Forest Dr, 65

Emerald View Ct, 65
Emily Cir, 110
Emmelman Rd, 75
Enclave Cir, 45
Enstrom Rd, 75
Epsom Dr W, 38
Equestrian Club Dr, 87, 97
Equestrian Dr, 99
Equestrian Way, 86, 87
Equine Ln, 99
Essex Ct, 31
Essex Dr, 66
Estancia Ln, 96
Estate Dr, 69, 70
Etna Dr, 55
Euston Ct, 42
Evening Star Way, 111, 118
Eventing St, 111
Everglades Way, 107
Exeter Estate Ln, 109
Exeter Ln, 65
Exotica Ln, 64, 65
F Rd, 17, 29, 41, 53
Fairdale Way, 63
Fairfield Ct, 67
Fairgrounds Rd, 45, 46, 57
Fairlane Ct, 87, 88
Fairlane Farms Rd, 90
Fairmont Village Dr, 108, 109
Fairway Cove Ct, 77
Fairway Island Dr, 90
Fairway Ln, 31
Fairway Ter, 33
Falcon Crane Way, 46
Falling Leaf Ln, 51
Falls St, 68
Fallview Way, 63

Fargo Ave, 92, 102
Farley Rd, 29
Farmington Ave, 65, 77
Farmington Cir, 77
Farmington Ct, 65
Farrier Pl, 52, 63, 64
Fascination Ln, 44
Fashion Pl, 110
Fatio Blvd, 81, 92
Fawn Dr, 12, 24
Fawnwood Pl, 66
Fernwood Cres, 54
Ferris Pl, 5
Fiddlewood Ct, 30
Fieldview Way, 98
Finch Ct, 32
Firethorn Dr, 64, 76
Firewood Ct, 65
Fishing Hawk Ln, 24
Fishpond Ct, 68
Flagler Estates Dr, 33
Flagler Manor Cir, 34, 46
Flagler Pkwy, 33, 45
Flamingo Rd, 28
Flora Ln, 64
Florence St, 91
Floridas Tpke, 103
Florida's Tpke, 58, 70, 82, 93, 103, 111, 118
Fly Rod Run, 35, 36
Flying Cow Rd, 51, 63, 75, 85, 86, 95
Foal Rd, 116
Folkstone Cir, 76, 77
Folkstone Ct, 77
Folsom Rd, 30, 42, 54
Fontana Ln, 18
Fontana Pl, 18
Forest Bent Blvd, 70
Forest Club Dr W, 65, 66
Forest Dale Dr, 109

Forest Glen Ln, 51, 63
Forest Hill Blvd, 54, 66, 78, 79, 80, 81, 82
Forest Ln, 39, 40
Forester Ct, 54
Foresteria Ave, 64
Fortner Dr, 15, 16
Fortune Cir, 90
Fortune Dr, 80
Fortune Way, 90
Fountain Rd, 110
Fountain View Blvd, 77, 88
Four Winds Rd, 66
Fox Ct, 80
Fox Trail Ln, 49, 50
Fox Trail Rd S, 32, 33
Fox Trl, 29
Fox View Ct, 34, 110
Fox View Pl, 102, 110
Freesian Way, 91
Fresh Creek, 34
Frontier Ave, 92, 102
Futana Way, 82
G Rd E, 18, 30
G Square Rd, 30
Galiano St, 31
Galicia St, 20
Galleon Dr, 33
Galleria, 68
Galleria St, 68
Gallop Dr, 25, 37
Galloway Trl, 76
Galoway Trl, 76
Garden Cress Trl, 44
Garden Ct, 43
Garden Point Trl, 96, 104
Gardenia Dr, 43, 55
Garibaldi Rd, 1, 11
Garwood Ct, 53

Gator Ln, 58
Gator Trl, 112
Gelding Ct, 116
Gem Twist Ct, 97
Gembrook Ct, 30
Gene Mische Way, 87, 97
Georgian Ct, 65
Geranium Pl, 76, 77
Gibraltar St, 19
Gibson Cay, 22
Gingerwood Ln, 66
Gisela Rd, 11
Glasgow Dr E, 26
Glasgow Dr W, 26
Glen Bay Dr, 78, 89
Glen Willow Ln, 51
Glendale Ct, 18
Glendale Dr, 18
Glendale Pl, 18
Glenfield Way, 69
Glidden Ct, 92
Global Trl, 5
Gloucester Ct, 66
Gold Cay, 22
Gold Piece Trl, 53, 65
Gold Tee Ct, 77
Goldcup Dr E, 26
Goldcup Dr W, 26
Golden Cypress Ct, 103
Golden Point Ln, 86
Golden River Dr, 46
Goldenrod Rd, 64, 65
Goldenwood Way, 66
Goldfinch Ln, 31
Golf Brook Dr, 79, 90
Golf Ln, 1
Goodwood Ter, 65
Gracida St, 97, 98
Granada St, 19, 20, 31, 32

Grand Duke Way, 44
Grand Lacuna Blvd, 118
Grand National Dr E, 38
Grand National Dr W, 38
Grand Oak Way, 80
Grand Oaks Blvd, 30
Grand Prix Farms Rd, 87, 97
Grand Prix Village Dr, 96, 97
Grande Blvd, 34
Grande Rd, 1, 11
Grandview Cir, 44
Grandview Ct, 44
Grandview Mnr, 100
Grandview Way, 44
Granite Ridge Ln, 69
Grantham Ct, 77
Grantham Dr, 65, 77
Grasmere Way, 109
Grassy Isle Trl, 117, 118
Gray Hawk Way, 110
Gray Mare Way, 76
Great Dane Ln, 17, 18
Great Egret Ct, 33
Green Cay, 22
Green Cypress Way, 103
Green Finch Ter, 65
Green Grove Ct, 1, 2
Green Turtle Ln, 70
Greenbriar Blvd, 75, 76, 77, 86, 87, 88
Greenbriar Cir, 79
Greenbriar Villa Dr, 109
Greenleaf Ln, 65
Greenshore Pl, 77
Greenspire Ln, 102
Greentree Dr, 64
Greentree Trl, 52, 53
Greenview Cove Dr, 77

Greenview Shores Blvd, 63, 64, 65, 77, 88
Greenway Cir S, 43
Greenway Dr, 43
Greenway Village N, 43
Greenwich Ln, 91
Greenwood Ct, 9
Greenwood Pl, 18
Grouse Ln, 43
Gruber Ln, 40
Grumman Ct, 86
Guadeloupe Dr, 82
Guava Ct, 64
Guilford Cir, 66
Guilford St, 65
Guilford Way, 66
Gulf Cove Dr, 110
Gulf Pine Cir, 51
Gulf Run Way, 110, 111
Gulf Sounds Ln, 110
Gulfstream Cir, 18
Gulfstream Dr, 18
Gulfstream Way, 33, 45
Gulls Nest, 31
Habitat Ct, 18
Hadjes Dr, 103
Haldin Pl, 8, 9
Hale Ct, 78
Halifax Ct, 77
Halter Rd, 64
Hamblin Way, 92
Hamilton Ter, 68
Handy Oak Cir, 46
Hanover Cir, 1, 2, 11, 12
Hanoverian Dr, 111
Harborside Cir, 78
Harbour Club Dr, 118
Harbour Greens Dr, 118
Harbour Oak Dr, 118
Harbour View Ct, 33
Harlena Dr E, 38

Harlena Dr W, 38
Harmony Way, 44
Harness Cir, 91, 101
Hartridge Ter, 92
Harwood Ln, 111, 118
Havasu Ct, 118
Hawk Hollow, 107, 108
Hawker Ln, 75
Hawthorne Pl, 64, 76
Haymarket Ct, 51, 52
Hayworth St, 77
Hazleton Ln, 108, 109
Headwater Cir, 66
Headwater Ter, 66
Headwater Way, 66
Heartwood Pl, 67
Heather Ct, 42
Heatherwood Dr, 31
Heathridge Dr, 45, 46
Heirloom Ln, 35, 36
Hemingway Ct, 30
Hempstead St, 66
Henley Pl, 77
Hermitage Dr, 82
Heron Cove Dr, 21, 33
Heron Pkwy, 31, 43
Herons Nest Ct, 116, 117
Hialeah Dr E, 4
Hialeah Dr W, 4
Hibiscus Dr, 43, 55
Hibiscus Ln, 54
Hickory, 66
Hickory Trl, 66
Hickstead Pl, 87
Hidden Bend Way, 80
Hidden Cypress Way, 103
Hidden Pine Dr, 54
Hidden Pine Ln, 54
Hidden Wood Dr, 54
Hideaway Bend, 65

High Cay, 34
Hiller St, 86
Hollow Tree Ln, 85, 86
Hollyhock Rd, 64, 76
Homeland Rd, 108, 115
Honey Oak Ct, 35
Honeytree Ln, 65
Honeywell Rd, 110
Hookline Cir, 35, 36
Hooks Rd, 103, 111
Hooper Rd, 58
Hope Bay, 34
Horicon Ct, 19
Horse Trl, 2
Horseshoe Trce, 52, 64
Howald Rd, 11
Hoylake Rd, 93
Hull Ct, 77
Hunter Dr, 80
Hunter Ln, 1, 105
Hunters Ct, 80
Hunting Trl, 102, 109, 110
Huntington Dr, 66, 67, 79
Huntley Way, 63
Hurlingham Dr, 88, 89
Hutton Blvd, 91, 92
Hyacinth Ct, 65
Hyacinth Pl, 65
Hyde Park Rd, 41
Ian Trl, 5
Ibisca Ter, 44
Imperial Club Ln, 100
Imperial Isle Dr, 100, 101
Imperial Point Ln, 86
Inagua Ln, 82
Indian Head Cir, 30, 31, 42

Indian Mound Rd, 95, 96, 97, 98, 99, 104
Indian Trail Dr, 19
Indigo Ave, 53, 65
Infanta Ave, 19
Infanta Ct, 19
Inverness Cir, 79
Inverness Rd, 103
Ira Ln, 108
Iron Forge Ct, 30, 42
Ishnala Cir, 53
Ishnala Ct, 53
Island Reef Dr, 100, 108
Isle Brook Ct, 90
Isles Blvd, 100
Isles View Dr, 100
Isles Vista Blvd, 100, 108
Isles Way S, 100
Isleworth Ct, 30
Isola Cir, 56
Italia Way, 102
Italian Cypress Way, 51
Ivanhoe, 90, 91
Ivanhoe Ln, 91
Ivy Dr, 65
Jacaranda Ct, 42
Jackpine St, 67
Jamboree Ct, 54
James Estate Ct, 101, 109
James Estate Ln, 101, 109
Jappeloup Ln, 97
Jay Ct, 44
Jenny Ln W, 26
Jewel Ln, 27
Jockey Rd, 116
Johnson Ln, 46
Jolly Harbour Ct, 82
Jonquil Ct, 65
Jonquil Pl, 65

Jumper Ln, 11
Jumper Rd, 105
Juniper Pl, 64
Kaliko Ln, 82
Kapok Cres, 42
Karanda Ct, 31
Kazee Rd, 18
Kelly Dr, 58
Kelty St, 117
Kelty Way, 117
Kemps Bay, 34
Kensington Park Way, 101, 109
Kensington Way, 56, 68
Kerry Ln, 29, 41
Key Deer Cir, 115
Keystone Ct, 68
King Fisher Ln, 11
King Ter, 76
Kingfisher Way, 31
Kinglet Ter, 67
Kings Way, 30, 42
Kingsbury Ct, 65
Kingsbury Dr, 65
Kingsbury Ter, 65
Kingsdale Ln, 66
Kingsmoor Way, 110, 111
Kingsway Rd, 78
Kinkaid Ter, 109
Kipling Way, 109
Klays Ct, 18
Knights Ct, 30
Knightsbridge Pl, 108
Knollwood Ct, 30, 42
Knotty Wood Ln, 53
Knoxwood Ct, 101
la Mancha Ave, 9, 10, 20, 32
la Mirada Cir, 53
Laborie Ln, 82

Lacewood Ln, 66
Lago de Talavera, 101, 102
Lago del Sol Dr, 116
Lake Breeze Ct, 78
Lake Breeze Dr, 65, 66
Lake Crystal Dr, 34, 46
Lake Cypress Rd, 103
Lake Isles Dr, 100
Lake Shore Dr, 80
Lake Susan Dr, 46
Lake Terry Dr, 46
Lake Victoria Dr, 46
Lake Wellington Dr, 65, 66
Lake Worth Rd, 98, 99, 100, 101, 102, 103
Lakefield North Ct, 63, 75
Lakepoint Ct, 117, 118
Lakeside Dr, 15
Lakeview Cir, 31
Lakeview Dr, 31
Lakeview Dr E, 31
Lakeview Dr W, 31
Lame Panther Ln, 2
Lamstein Ln, 43, 55
Lancashire Dr E, 14
Lancashire Dr W, 14
Lancaster Way, 68
Lantana Rd, 115, 116, 117, 118
Lantern Bay Cir, 33
Lantern Dr, 110
Lantern Tree Ln, 66
Larch Way, 67
Laredo Way, 107, 114
Larkspur Ln, 64
Las Brisas Ct, 79
Las Casitas Ct, 79
Las Casitas Dr, 79

Las Palmas Ave, 105
Las Palmas St, 9, 10, 19, 20
Lasso Way, 107, 114
Latina Pl, 75
Laurel Estates Ln, 101
Laurel Estates Way, 101
Laurel Trl, 87
Laurel Valley Cir, 67, 79
Laurel Walk Rd, 100
Laurel Way, 18
Lavender Ln, 65
Learwood Dr, 2
Leeds Ct, 78
Legend Lake Dr, 109
Lemongrass Ln, 64
Lewes St, 78
Lexington Dr, 18
Lexington Pl, 18
Lilac Dr, 43
Lilac Pl, 65, 77
Lily Ct, 64
Lime Dr, 80, 91
Linda Ct, 43
Lindbergh Ln, 86
Linden Way, 118
Lindsey Ct, 77
Lineyard Cay, 34
Linkside Dr, 77, 88
Linnet Ln, 31
Lion Country Safari Rd, 13, 14, 25, 37, 49
Lion Trl, 25
Lisbon Ct, 75
Little Mustang Way, 116
Little Pine Ln, 102
Little Ranches Trl, 55
Little Rock Ct, 77
Llama Ln, 25
Lockheed Ter, 75
Locust Ln, 42, 43

Long Bay, 34
Long Bow Ct, 43
Long Meadow Dr, 90
Longlea Ter, 63
Longleaf Ln, 91
Longwood Green Dr, 78, 79
Longwood Green Dr W, 78
Los Angeles Dr, 39
Lotus Ln, 76
Love Cres, 19
Loxahatchee Ave, 52
Lucca St, 91
Lynbrook Ct, 42
Lynton Cir, 77, 78
Lynx Pl, 24
Lyons Rd, 58, 70, 82, 92, 93, 102, 110, 117
Lytham Ct, 46
Mabillon Way, 101
Macadamia Ct, 43
Madewood Ct, 57, 69
Madison Chase, 46
Madrid St, 19, 20
Mahogany Ln, 58
Mahoris Dr, 19
Maidstone Dr, 78, 79
Mainsail Ct, 108
Malaga St, 9, 10
Malbec Way, 80
Mallard Ct, 31
Mallet Cir, 78, 89
Mallet Hill Ct, 88
Man of War, 34
Manatee Bay Ln, 108
Manchester Lake Dr, 101
Manchineel Ct, 31
Mancho Way, 103
Mandarin Blvd, 3, 13

Manderly Dr, 108
Manderly Ln, 108
Mandeville Ln, 42
Mango Blvd, 9
Mangrove Cay, 34
Mangrove Ct, 54
Manjack Cay, 34
Mantova Dr, 116, 117
Marble Canyon Dr, 53, 65
Marblestone Ct, 79
Marcella Blvd, 41, 42
March Cir, 17, 18, 29
Mare Ln, 37
Margate Pl, 78
Marginada Way, 110
Marginal Rd, 58, 70
Margo Way, 2
Marigold Dr, 76, 77
Marina Bay Rd, 108
Mariners Cove Dr, 100, 108
Mariposa Grove Cir, 58
Maritime Ct, 108
Marsh Hawk Ln, 24
Marsh St, 68
Marsh Wren Ct, 110, 117
Marshwood Ln, 118
Marston Ln, 111
Martin Cir, 32, 44
Mastic Cay, 22
Mastic Tree Ct, 31
Mayacoo Club Dr, 45
Mayacoo Lakes Blvd, 45
Mayfair Dr E, 14
Mayfair Dr W, 14
Mayorca Ct, 19
Mayview Way, 63
Mc Dermott Ln, 44
McAllister Way, 58

McAneeny Ct, 92
Mead Hill Dr E, 4
Mead Hill Dr W, 4
Meadow Ave, 64
Meadow Wood Dr, 63
Meadow Woode Ct, 54
Meadow Woode Dr, 54, 55
Meadowbend Dr, 78
Meadowbreeze Dr, 65, 66, 77, 78
Meadowland Dr, 66, 77, 78
Meadowlands Dr, 18
Meadowlark Dr, 31, 43
Meander Cir, 43
Medical Park Blvd, 80
Medicis Pl, 101
Mellow Ct, 9, 10
Melody Rd, 110
Menorca Ct, 63
Merion Ct, 67
Merriweather Way, 81
Michlar Dr, 108, 115
Mid Pines Ter, 53
Middleburg Dr, 98
Midship Way, 33
Midsummer Ct, 30, 31
Mikado Ln, 44, 45
Milan Ct, 75
Milford Ct, 78
Mill Pond Ln, 54
Mimosa St, 9
Miramar Ave, 19
Miramontes Cir, 99, 100
Misty Ln, 44
Misty Oaks Cir, 18
Misty Shores Way, 33
Mizner Lake Ct, 78, 89
Mizner Way, 78, 88, 89
Mohawk Dr, 19

Monroe St, 78
Montauk Dr, 66, 78
Montclaire Ct, 69
Monterey Way, 8
Montserrat Pl, 93
Moon Bay Cir, 100
Moonflower Cir, 77
Moonlight Way, 44
Moonrise Dr, 118
Moonstone Ter, 65
Morgan Close, 52
Morgans Blf, 34
Morgate Cir, 42
Morning Glory Dr, 64, 65
Morning Mist Way, 109, 116
Morning Star Rd, 111, 118
Morrow Ct, 27
Moss Pointe Cir, 102
Mourning Dove Ln, 65
Moxey Pt, 22
Mozart Rd, 57, 69
Muir Cir, 78, 89
Muirfield Ct, 90
Mulberry Grove Rd, 57
Mulberry Pl, 65
Murray Ln, 12, 13
Myakka Ct, 118
Mystic Ct, 66
Mystic Way, 66
N 145th Ave, 6
N 162nd Dr, 4, 14, 26, 38
N Bight, 22
N Blairwood Cir, 118
N San Andros, 22
N State Rd 7, 33, 45, 57
Nantucket Bay Ct, 100
Narragansett Bay Ct, 100

Narrowleaf Ct, 31, 42, 43
Natchez Ct, 19
Natchez Trace Ave, 19
Natures Point Ln, 86
Natures Way, 18
Nautica Ct, 100
Neaton Ct, 75, 86
Netherlee Way, 101
Nevis Pl, 93
New Castle Ter, 65
New Haven Ave, 77, 78
New Hope Ct, 57, 69
New Kent Ct, 43
Newberry Ln, 68
Newbury Ct, 77
Newbury Dr, 77
Newhaven Lake Dr, 101
Newhaven Point Ln, 69, 81
Newquay Ct, 75
Newton Pl, 78
Newton Way, 118
Niantic Ter, 66
Nicholls Pt, 22
Norris Rd, 85
North Rd, 5, 6, 7, 17, 18
Northampton Ter, 66
Northgate Ct, 31
Northgreen Dr, 100, 101
Northshire Trl, 65
Northumberland Cir, 65
Northumberland Ct, 65
Norwick St, 87, 88
Nottingham Rd, 42
Nucare Ln, 91
Nugent Trl, 33, 34
Nuvista Ave, 91
Oak Alley Dr, 117
Oak Bend Way, 68, 80
Oak Berry Cir, 80

Oak Chase Ct, 51
Oak Chase Dr, 51
Oak Hamlet Ln, 80
Oak Ln, 31
Oak Meadow Ln, 109
Oak Shadow Way, 66
Oakmont Dr, 93
Oakmont Estates Blvd, 91
Oakton Preserve Way, 34
Oakwater Dr, 30, 31
Oatland Ct, 75, 76
Ocean Breeze Ln, 96
Oceanaire Way, 118
Ocho Rios Ln, 93
Odessa Trl, 65
Okeechobee Blvd, 27, 28, 29, 30, 31, 32, 33, 34
Okeechobee Blvd E, 26, 27
Okeechobee Blvd W, 26
Okeeheelee Park, 70, 82
Old Clydesdale Cir, 116
Old Country Rd, 54, 66
Old Crestwood Blvd, 54
Old Cypress Trl, 67, 79
Old Englishtown Rd, 65
Old Hammock Way, 68
Old Hampton Dr, 86, 87, 96, 97
Old Lighthouse Cir, 100
Old Oak Ct, 63
Old Winston Ct, 116
Oleander Dr, 55
Oleaster Ave, 53, 65
Oliver Ln, 44
Olmstead Dr, 110
Olympia Blvd, 81
Oneida Ter, 53

Opal Ln, 65
Orange Ave, 52
Orange Grove Blvd, 4, 7, 8, 9, 10
Orchid Ct, 65
Orchid Dr, 43, 55
Oriole Ct, 43
Osley Farms Rd, 51
Osprey Pointe Cir, 99, 100
Ottawa Ct, 30, 31
Otter Run, 107, 108
Ouachita Dr, 111, 118
Ousley Sod Farm Rd, 104
Oxen Hill Ct, 30, 31
Oxford Ct, 30
Pacer Cir, 52
Pacifica St, 100
Paddle Foot, 17
Paddock Dr, 52, 53, 64
Palais Ter, 101
Palisades Dr, 34
Palisades Lakes Dr, 34
Palladium Pl, 110
Palm Beach Plantation Blvd, 57, 58
Palm Beach Point Blvd, 86, 96, 97, 104, 105
Palm Beach Trace Dr, 31
Palm Breeze Trl, 96
Palm Cove Ln, 66
Palm Dale Rd Exn, 46
Palm Deer Dr, 12, 24
Palm Ln, 54
Palma Ln, 96
Palmetto Ln, 54
Palms West Dr, 53, 54
Palms West Pkwy, 53
Palomino Dr, 101, 102, 103
Pampas Way, 63

Pancho Way, 103
Par Dr, 19
Paradise Cove Ln, 108
Paradise Cres, 19
Paradise Trl, 28
Park Central, 54
Park Forest Way, 66
Park Rd N, 42, 43
Park Rd S, 42
Parkwood, 19
Parkwood Dr, 19
Parkwood Dr S, 19
Partridge Ln, 31
Paseo Ct, 19
Paso Fino Dr, 90, 91, 101
Patience Ln, 44, 45
Paw Paw Cay, 22
Payson Way, 92
Pebble Beach Ct, 103
Pebble Beach Dr, 93, 103
Pebble Ridge Ln, 69
Pebblewood Dr, 79
Peconic Ct, 66, 78
Peel Ct, 65
Pekoe Ter, 65
Pelham Cir, 106
Pelham Rd, 64
Pelican Bay Ct, 100
Pelican Dr, 80
Penhale Ct, 87
Pennington Ct, 30
Pennypacker Trl, 65
Penzance Ln, 44, 45
Pepper Tree Cres, 42, 43
Peppergrass Run, 44, 56
Peppertree Ct, 66
Periwinkle Pl, 64
Perkins Dr, 41, 42
Perserve Ct, 30, 42
Perserve Way, 42

Perth Rd, 117
Petrel Rd, 67
Phipps Ln, 92
Picasso Ct, 42
Pienza Cir, 20
Pierside Cir, 78
Pierson Rd, 86, 87, 88, 89, 90
Pigeon Cay, 34
Pillsbury Way, 92
Pimlico Dr E, 14
Pimlico Dr W, 14
Pimlico Way, 18
Pinafore Ln, 44, 45
Pine Cay, 22, 34
Pine Cay Rd, 93
Pine Chase Ct, 51
Pine Club Ln, 51
Pine Dust Ct, 101, 102
Pine Ln, 31
Pine Mill Ct, 102
Pine Pl, 18
Pine Rd, 18
Pine Run Ct, 101
Pine Shadow Way, 54, 66
Pine Strand Ct, 63
Pine Trail Ct, 102
Pine Valley Dr, 67
Pineacre Ct, 54
Pineacre Ln, 54
Pineapple Dr, 52
Pineland Rd, 69
Pinelands Cir, 108
Pinetta Cir, 67
Pineville Dr, 117
Pinion Dr, 92, 93
Pintail Ct, 31
Pintail Dr, 67
Pinto Cir, 52, 64
Pinto Ct, 52

Pinto Dr, 102, 103
Pinto Palm Ct, 31
Pioneer Ln, 58, 70
Pioneer Rd, 57, 58, 68, 69
Pioneer Way, 69
Piper Rdg, 31
Piper Way, 86
Piping Plover Rd, 114, 115
Pipit Ct, 67
Pippin Ln, 44
Pisa Rd, 91
Pitrizza Dr, 102, 103
Placid Ter, 111
Plantation Estates Dr, 57
Playa Dr, 93
Players Ct, 78, 89
Pleasant Wood Dr, 54
Pleasure Dr E, 4
Pleasure Dr W, 4
Plum Cay, 22
Poinciana Blvd, 43
Polo Club Dr, 88
Polo Club Rd, 77, 78, 79, 88, 89, 90
Polo Gardens Dr, 78
Polo Island Dr, 88
Polo Lake Dr E, 80
Polo Lake Dr W, 80
Polo Lakes Blvd, 80
Polo Ln, 11
Polo Rd, 103, 111
Polo Rd E, 88
Polo Rd W, 88
Pomerol Dr, 80
Ponce de Leon St, 19, 31
Pond Bluff Ct, 117
Pond View Dr, 79
Ponderosa Ct, 42
Pony Run, 91, 101

Portasol Ave, 20, 32
Portland Ave, 78
Portland Ct, 78
Positano Way, 117
Postley Ct, 92
Powell Rd, 33
Prado Blvd, 13, 14
Prado St, 9
Prarieview Dr, 11, 23
Prato St, 91
Preakness Dr E, 14
Preakness Dr W, 14
Preserve Dr, 30, 42
Prestige Dr, 31
Prestwich Dr E, 14
Prestwich Dr W, 14
Primrose Ln, 64, 76
Princess Ct, 30
Princeton, 90
Princeton Ct, 42
Professional Way, 51
Puffin Ct, 44
Purslane Ter, 65
Pyes Harbour, 22, 34
Quail Rd, 41
Quarry Rd, 117
Quarter Horse Trl, 87, 88
Quaye Lake Cir, 69
Quaye Side Dr, 69
Quaye View Way, 68, 69
Quebec Ct, 30
Queens Ln, 30
Quercus Ct, 54
Quercus Ln, 54
Quiet Woods Rd, 65
Quill Cir, 102
Quincy Ct, 30
Quinn Ct, 92
Quito Pl, 93
Raceway Rd, 116
Rachel Ln, 69

Rackley Rd, 42
Rainbow Springs Ter, 43
Rainforest Ct, 8
Raintree Ln, 64
Ramblewood Cir, 43
Rambling Drive Cir, 55, 67
Ranchwood Ct, 51, 52
Randi Dr, 78
Range Line Rd, 33, 45, 56, 57, 68, 80, 91, 101, 109, 116
Raven Ct, 32
Raymond Dr, 41, 42
Reading Ter, 65
Rearing Ln, 111
Red Bay, 34
Red Parrot Ln, 65
Red Pine Trl, 67, 79
Redondo Way, 53
Regal Ct, 78
Regal Ct E, 78
Regal Ct N, 78
Regal Ct S, 78
Regal Ct W, 78
Regalo Dr, 20
Regatta Ln, 108
Reids Cay, 22
Rembrandt Blvd, 50
Rene Lacoste Pl, 79
Reptile Pass, 25
Reston Cir, 30, 31
Reynolds Rd, 108, 115
Rhapsody Way, 44
Rhino Rd, 25
Rhythm Cir, 44
Ridgeback Run, 70
Ridgefield Dr, 30
Ridgewood Cir, 18, 30
Ridgewood Dr, 118
Ring Rd, 80, 91

Rio Claro Dr N, 93
Rio Claro Dr S, 93
Ripley Run, 80
River Bluff Ln, 43
River Run St, 31
Rivera Ave, 9
Rivera Ct, 9
Riverside Cir, 66
Roan Ct, 75, 76
Roberts Way, 39, 40
Roche Pl, 92
Rockville Ln, 18
Rodeo Dr, 102, 103
Rolling Meadows Cir, 63
Rolling Rock Pl, 75, 76
Rolling Rock Trl, 76
Rosalie Ln, 93
Rose Bay Ct, 43
Rose Ct, 64
Roselle Ct, 31
Roselynn Way, 115
Rosemont Dr, 117
Rosetta Trl, 70
Rosewood Ln, 65
Rowayton Cir, 66
Royal Cardigan Way, 81
Royal Commerce Rd, 55
Royal Cove Way, 66
Royal Ct, 42
Royal Cypress Ln, 103
Royal Devon Dr, 101, 109
Royal Devon Rd, 100, 101
Royal Devon Way, 100, 109
Royal Fern Blvd, 79
Royal Palm Beach Blvd, 9, 19, 31, 43, 55
Royal Pine Cir E, 19
Royal Pine Cir N, 19

Royal Pine Cir S, 19
Royal Pine Cir W, 19
Royal Plaza Rd, 55
Royalle Ter, 101
Roycourt Cir, 19
Rudder Cv, 66
Running Oak Ct, 30
Running Oak Ln, 30
Rustic Rd, 74, 75
Ryan Ln, 44
Rye Ter, 76
S 125th Ave, 99, 107
S Andover Coach Ln, 101
S Blairwood Cir, 118
S Breeze Pl, 100
S Canal Cir, 118
S Club Dr, 63, 75
S Crown Way, 90
S Florida Water Management Science Rd, 118
S Rambling Dr, 67
S San Andros, 34
S Sea Ct, 100
S Shore Blvd, 77, 78, 79, 88, 98, 106, 113
Sabal Ct, 54
Sabal Tree Ct, 34
Sachem Head Ter, 66
Saddle Club Way, 105
Saddle Ct, 109, 110
Saddle Ranch Rd, 111
Saddle Trail Ln, 116
Saddle Trl, 19
Saddlebrook Dr, 80
Safari Cir, 25
Safe Haven Dr, 58, 70
Sag Harbor Ct, 78
Sage Ave, 64
Sage Meadow Trl, 44
Sailboat Cir, 66

Sailfish Cove Dr, 33
Saint Davids Ct, 54
Saint Davids Way, 54
Saint Emma Dr, 57, 69
Salerno Dr, 117
Sallys Aly, 27
Salzedo St, 9
Samoset Ct, 53
San Andros, 22, 34
San Diego Dr, 39
San Fratello Cir, 111
San Lorenzo Way, 91
Sand Drift Way, 45
Sand Lake Ct, 117, 118
Sand Pine Way, 19
Sanderling Dr, 67
Sandpiper Ave, 31, 43
Sandpiper Ln, 33
Sandpiper Shores Way, 33
Sandstone Ct, 77
Sandstone Ridge Ct, 69
Sandy Cay, 22, 34
Sandy Cove Ter, 111
Sandy Creek Way, 111
Sandy Ln, 19
Sandy Pine Ct, 54
Sannenwood Ln, 66
Sansburys Way, 34, 46, 58
Santa Barbara Dr, 88
Santa Clara Trl, 53, 65
Santa Cruz Ave, 9
Santa Monica Ave, 19
Santa Monica Ct, 19
Santander Ct, 9
Santiago St, 19, 31
Sapphire Cir, 33
Sapphire Cove Dr, 33
Saratoga Blvd E, 18, 19
Saratoga Blvd W, 8, 18

Sarita Ct, 31
Sarona Cir, 44
Savoyard Way, 44
Sawgrass Ct, 54, 66
Sawyer Ter, 91, 92
Scarborough Ter, 53
Schweizer Ct, 86
Scott Pl, 39, 40
Scribner Ln, 91, 92
Sea Chase Dr, 111
Sea Lavender Ter, 53, 65
Sea Mist Ln, 86
Sea Mist Way, 100
Seaford Dr, 77, 78
Seagull Ct, 32
Seagull Park Dr N, 45
Seagull Park Dr S, 45
Secretariat Dr E, 26
Secretariat Dr W, 26
Segovia Ave, 19
Segovia Ct, 19
Segura St, 9
Seminole Ct E, 19
Seminole Ct W, 19
Seminole Dr, 19
Seminole Lake Dr, 43
Seminole Lakes Dr, 43
Seminole Palms Dr, 55
Seminole Pratt Whitney
   Rd, 4, 14, 26, 38, 50
Seneca Ct, 19
Serenade Cir, 44
Serenade Ln, 44
Sevilla Ave, 19
Shady Pines Ct, 66
Shaker Cir, 66, 78, 79
Shakerwood Ln, 78, 79
Shamrock Dr, 27
Shaughnessy Dr, 91, 92
Shawmut Ct, 53
Shearson Blvd, 81, 82

Sheffield Ct, 87
Sheffield St, 87, 88
Sheffield Woods Dr, 65
Sheila Ct, 80
Sheltingham Dr, 90
Shepard Pl, 80, 81
Sheridan Ter, 65
Sherwood Dr, 19
Shetland Ln, 37, 38
Shoma Dr, 56, 68
Shoma Ln, 56, 68
Shoreline Dr, 78
Shoreside Cir, 78
Shoreside Ln, 78
Showboat Ln, 44
Shower Tree Way, 79
Shutterfly Way, 96
Sicily Ter, 75
Siena Cir, 90, 91
Silent Oak Cir, 69
Silk Carnation Way, 56
Silver Bell Cres, 54
Silver Glen Dr, 100
Silver Glen Way, 110
Silver Ridge St, 100
Silverbell Ln, 65
Simonson Dr, 80, 81
Skipiks Way, 85
Skipton Ave, 65
Skyhawk Ln, 23
Sloane Pl, 80, 81
Snail Trl, 28
Snapdragon Dr, 64
Snowbell Pl, 65
Snowberry Dr, 64
Softwood Ct, 63
Sonata Way, 44
Song Sparrow Ln, 65
Sorrel Ln, 25
South Rd, 97, 105

Southern Blvd, 47, 48,
   49, 50, 51, 52, 53, 54,
   55, 56, 57, 58
Southern Pride Pl, 91
Southfields Rd, 88, 98
Southport Ct, 66
Spanish Moss Rd E, 102
Spanish Moss Rd W, 102
Spanish Oak Way, 67
Spanish Pine Ter, 19
Spanish Wells, 34
Sparrow Ct, 43
Sparrow Dr, 31, 32, 42,
   43
Sparrow Ln, 43
Sparrow Pl, 43
Sparrow Ter, 43
Spinnaker Ct, 66
Spinnaker Ln, 66
Spinnaker Rd, 66
Split Rail Run, 35
Spr Close, 52
Spray Dr, 45
Spring Crest Ct, 103
Spring Wheat Rdg, 23
Springdale Rd, 103
Springhill Ct, 63
Springwood Pl, 67
Squire Dr, 51, 52, 63, 64
St Andrews Pl, 78, 79
St Andrews Rd, 103
St Germain Ct, 101
St Johns Ct, 93
Stables Way, 105
Staghorn Ct, 65
Staghorn St, 65
Staimford Cir, 77
Staimford Ct, 77
Staimford Dr, 77
Stallion Dr, 25, 37
Stallion Dr E, 26

Stallion Dr W, 26
Stamford Ave, 31
Staniel Cay, 22
Stapleton Way, 63
Star Clusters Ct, 31
Stardust Way, 44
Starling Ave, 32, 44
State Hwy 7, 33, 45, 56,
   57, 68, 80, 91, 101,
   109, 116
State Hwy 704, 33, 34
State Hwy 80, 47, 48, 49,
   50, 51, 52, 53, 54, 55,
   56, 57, 58
State Hwy 802, 101, 102,
   103
State Hwy 812, 115, 116,
   117, 118
State Hwy 882, 78, 79,
   80, 81, 82
State Hwy 91, 58, 70, 82,
   93, 103, 111, 118
State Rd 7, 10, 20, 21,
   33, 57
Steffan Ln, 15, 16
Sterling Pine Pl, 35
Stinson Way, 46
Stirrup Ln, 19, 52, 64
Stone Creek St, 100
Stone Pine Way, 54
Stonegate Dr, 77
Stonehaven Estates Dr,
   68, 69, 81
Stonington Ter, 33
Stonybrook Dr, 80
Stotesbury Way, 81
Stover Way, 91, 92
Strada Ct, 32
Stratford Creek, 34
Stratford St, 66
Strathmore Dr, 43

Strathmore Gate Dr, 31, 43
Streng Ln, 8, 18
Stribling Way, 79, 90, 91, 92
Stroller Way, 87
Sturbridge Ln, 67, 78, 79
Suellen Cir, 78, 79
Suffolk Dr, 18
Sugar Beach Way, 108
Sugar Pine Trl, 66
Sugarcane Ln, 115
Sugarwood Cres, 42, 43
Sulky Way, 54, 66
Summer Chase Ct, 103
Summer Creek Dr, 103
Summertime Ln, 44
Summerwood Cir, 67
Sunderland Ave, 77
Sunflower Cir, 9
Sunflower Ct, 65
Sunflower St, 9
Sunny Dr, 79
Sunnydale Dr, 78
Sunnyland Ln, 86, 96
Sunrise View Ln, 100, 108
Sunset Ln, 96
Sunset Point Cir, 78
Sunset Point Ct, 78
Sunset Point Dr, 78
Sunset Point Ln, 78
Sunshine Blvd, 19
Sunshine Rd, 57
Sunward St, 75
Swan Pkwy E, 31, 43
Swan Pkwy W, 31, 43
Swansea Ln, 33
Sweet Bay Ln, 42
Sweet Briar Pl, 65, 66
Sweet Wood Way, 66

Sweetgrass St, 35
Sweetwater Bnd, 31
Sword Fern Pl, 51
Sycamore Dr, 42
Sycamore Dr E, 4
Sycamore Dr W, 1, 2, 3, 4
Sycamore Ln, 66
Symphony Ln, 44
Take Off Pl, 75
Talbot Blvd, 102
Tally Ho Ln, 57, 58
Tamarack Way, 79
Tamis Trl, 108, 109
Tanbark Trl, 52
Tangerine Dr, 52, 53
Taormina St, 117
Teakwood Ct, 66
Teal Ct, 32
Tealwood Dr, 111
Tecoma Dr, 76
Temple Dr, 52
Tennis Court Way, 102
Tern Ct, 67
The 12th Fairway, 66, 67, 79
Thomas, 28
Thomas Ct, 28
Thomson Way, 81
Thorn Apple Ct, 31
Thornbank Ln, 44
Thornridge Ln, 44
Thoroughbred Run, 91
Thousand Pines Cir, 34
Thousand Pines Ct, 34
Thousand Pines Dr, 34
Tilden Pl, 79
Timber Pine Trl, 54
Timber Reap Trl, 35
Timber Ridge Cir, 66
Timberlane Pl, 39, 40

Tobago Ln, 93
Toledo St, 9
Torchwood Ct, 79
Torino Dr, 116, 117
Tornelia Ln, 64
Torrington Ave, 65
Tortoise Cv, 31
Toucan Trace Rd, 25
Touch of Class Ct, 97
Towing Ln, 89
Trace Ct, 19
Trace Way, 52, 64
Trafalgar Dr E, 14
Trafalgar Dr W, 14
Treanor Ter, 92
Treasure Cay, 34
Tree Stand Ter, 35
Treehaven Ct, 76
Trianon Pl, 101
Tripp Rd N, 16
Trotter Ct, 76
Tulip Ln, 77
Tumbleweed Ct, 66
Turenne Way, 101
Turf Ln, 64
Turnstone Dr, 67
Tuscany Dr, 44
Twig Rd, 109, 110
Twin Lakes Way, 8
Twin Oaks Way, 90
Tylerwood Ct, 66
Umbrella Cay, 34
Upper Cove Dr, 66
US Hwy 441, 47, 48, 49, 50, 51, 52, 53, 54, 55, 56, 57, 68, 80, 91, 101, 109, 116
US Hwy 98, 47, 48, 49, 50, 51, 52, 53, 54, 55, 56, 57, 58
Ushant Ct, 93

Valencia Dr, 52
Valencia St, 19
Valerian Way, 65
Valley Park Way, 102
Van Gogh Blvd, 38
Van Gogh Way, 30, 42
Vanderbilt Dr, 91
Vedado Ct, 19
Velazquez Blvd, 38
Velda Way, 63
Venetian Ln, 8
Venice Blvd, 44
Verdmont Ln, 93
Veronica Ct, 64
Versailles Blvd, 100, 101
Via Allegro, 81
Via Aurelia, 31
Via Bellezza, 82
Via Brilliante, 81, 82
Via Buena Vida, 81
Via Castello, 81
Via Christina, 98, 99
Via Classico E, 81
Via Classico W, 81
Via Elegante, 81
Via Emilia, 31
Via Fiore, 81
Via Grande E, 81, 82
Via Grande W, 81
Via Grandezza E, 81
Via Grandezza W, 81
Via Prestigo E, 82
Via Prestigo W, 81, 82
Via Prima, 82
Via Primo St, 116, 117
Via Toscana, 65
Via Veneto, 65
Vicara Ct, 20, 32
Victoria Grove Bend, 68
Victoria Pt, 22, 34
Vignon Ct, 101

Village Walk Dr, 43
Villagewalk Blvd, 93
Villagewalk Cir, 82, 92, 93
Vinings Cir, 78
Vinnings Cir, 78
Viscaya Ave, 9
Vista del Prado Dr, 79, 90
Vista Greens Ct, 102, 103
Voyageurs Pl, 63
W A Rd, 15
W Alan Black Blvd, 13, 14
W Aquaduct Dr, 14
W Arch Dr, 111
W Blairwood Cir, 118
W C Rd, 28, 40
W Canal Cir, 111, 118
W Citrus Dr, 52, 53
W Coconut Dr, 111
W Cornwall Dr, 26
W Cypress Rd, 111
W D Rd, 40, 52
W Epsom Dr, 38
W Fontana Ct, 18
W G Rd, 18, 30
W Greenway Dr, 43
W Lancashire Dr, 14
W Mango Rd, 111
W Palm Ave, 111
W Palmetto Rd, 111
W Pine Tree Ave, 111
W Plumosa Ln, 111
W Rambling Dr, 55, 67
W Rubber Tree Dr, 111
Waburton Ter, 81
Waccamaw Ln E, 111, 118
Wakulla Springs Way, 43

Waldorf Dr, 30
Waldorf St, 30
Wallis Rd, 58
Walnut Hill Dr, 117
Wandering Willow Way, 35
Wareham Ct, 87, 88
Warm Springs Ter, 53
Warner Ln, 81
Water Cay, 34
Waterbend Ct, 100
Watercress Ct, 91
Waterside Ct E, 80
Waterside Ct W, 80
Waterview Way, 54
Waterway Cove Dr, 66
Waterway Dr, 66, 67
Waterway Rd, 30, 42
Wax Wing Ter, 65
Weather Vane Pl, 78
Weatherly Rd, 75
Wellington Edge Blvd, 80
Wellington Green Dr, 80, 91
Wellington Lakes Blvd, 78
Wellington Parc Dr, 101
Wellington Preserve Blvd, 106, 107, 113, 114
Wellington Shores Dr, 100
Wellington Trce, 54, 64, 65, 66, 67, 76, 78, 79
Wellington View Dr, 69, 70
Wellington's Edge Blvd, 80
Wendy Cir, 70
Wendy Ln E, 70, 82

Wendy Ln N, 70
Wendy Ln S, 82
Wendy Ln W, 70, 82
Werwood Ct, 88
West Ct, 43
Westbury Close, 52
Westchester Ave, 65
Westecunk Dr, 19
Westhall Pl, 66
Westhampton Cir, 66, 78
Westmont Dr, 18, 19
Westmont Ln, 18, 19
Westmont Pl, 19
Westport Cir, 66
Westside Way, 44
Westwood Cir E, 57, 69
Westwood Cir N, 57
Westwood Cir W, 57, 69
Weybridge, 30
Weybridge Cir, 30, 31
Whale Boat Way, 100
Wheelbarrow Bnd, 35
Whimbrel Rd, 67
Whippoorwill Blvd, 69
Whippoorwill Isle N, 69
Whippoorwill Isle S, 69
Whippoorwill Pass, 69
Whippoorwill Row, 69
Whippoorwill Ter, 69
Whippoorwill Trl, 69
Whippoorwill Way, 69
Whispering Oak Cir, 58
Whispering Oak Trl, 58
Whispering Oak Way, 58
Whispering Willow Dr, 51
Whitby St, 78
Whitcombe Dr, 8, 9
White Cay, 22
White Coral Ct, 78

White Coral Dr, 78
White Coral Way, 78
White Cypress Dr, 118
White Egret Way, 111, 118
White Pine Dr, 66, 67
White Pinto Ct, 116
White Sands Cv, 117, 118
Whitehorse Dr, 91
Whitemarsh Dr, 67
Whitewood Cv E, 111
Whitewood Cv N, 111
Whitewood Cv S, 118
Whitewood Way, 111, 118
Whitney Way, 87
Whitton Dr E, 26
Widener Ter, 81
Widgeon Rd, 67
Wightman Dr, 79
Wild Cat Way, 32
Wild Cherry Ln, 65
Wild Oats, 31
Wild Orchid Trl, 115
Wild Pine Rd, 54
Wildebeast Way, 25
Williams Dr, 39, 40
Willow Basin Way, 111
Willow Cove Ln, 111
Willow Oak Ct, 90, 91
Willow Run Way, 110
Willow Sound Dr, 110
Willow Spring Dr, 103
Willow Springs Dr, 103
Willow Way, 18
Wiltshire Dr W, 26
Wiltshire Village Dr, 65, 77
Wimbledon Cir, 79
Windflower Ct, 64

Winding Oak Ln, 90
Winding Pearl Way, 100
Winding Woods Dr, 102
Windjammer Way, 33
Windmill Rd, 1
Windorah Way, 34, 46
Window Rock Dr, 53
Windship Cir, 65, 66, 78
Windsock Way, 75
Windsor Bay Pl, 108
Windsor Way Ct, 79, 90
Windtree Way, 66
Windward Cove Ln, 107, 108
Windwood Ln, 18
Wingate Bnd, 78
Winnipesankee Way, 111
Winnipesaukee Way, 111, 118
Winter Springs Ln, 103
Winter Wren Way, 110, 117
Winterhaven Cir, 69
Wisteria St, 77
Wither Close, 64
Wokker Dr, 102, 110
Wolcott Pl, 81
Wood Dale Dr, 54, 66
Wood Dale Ter, 63
Wood Glen Cir, 33
Wood Pine Ct, 102
Wood Rose Ct, 43
Wood Row Way, 63
Woodberry Ct, 102
Woodmar Ct, 63
Woodpecker Ct, 24
Woods Landing Trl, 70
Woods Walk Blvd, 101, 102
Woodwind Ln, 116, 117

Woodworth Ct, 81
Woolworth Ct, 80, 81
World Cup Ln, 99
Worswick Ct, 81
Wranglewood Dr, 54, 66
Wrevham Ct, 77
Wrotham Ter, 76, 77
Wychmere Ter, 53
Wycliffe Country Club Blvd, 101, 109
Wyeth Ct, 81
Wyndcliff Dr, 67, 79
Xanthus Ln, 93
Yachtman Pl, 66, 78
Yarmouth Ave, 77
Yarmouth Ct, 77
Yarmouth Dr, 77, 87, 88
Yearling Dr, 92, 93
Yellow Legs Lndg, 115
Yeoman Ln, 44, 45
Yerba Buena Ct, 118
York Ct, 76
Yorke Rd, 93
Yorkshire Dr E, 4
Yorkshire Dr W, 4
Zanzibar Ln, 93
Zebra Run Rd, 25

Made in the USA
Coppell, TX
17 November 2022

86547714R00077